I0441355

CYPRUS, PERMANENT DEPRIVATION OF FREEDOM

ISBN: 978-1-291- 50833-8

Andreas Sofroniou   2013 ©   Copyright

Andreas Sofroniou   2013 ©   Copyright

CYPRUS, PERMANENT DEPRIVATION OF FREEDOM

ISBN: 978-1-291- 50833-8

CONTENTS   PAGE:

1. CYPRUS DEPRIVED OF INDEPENDENCE

CYPRUS STRATEGICALLY POSITIONED IN THE MIDDLE

The geographical position of the island of Cyprus never allowed her to be free, nor will it ever be self-governed under the present European Union's approach to the island's political situation and its people's financial problems.

Cyprus is a small island and can easily be bullied by the mighty Northern European countries. As Cyprus is not important enough for the Southern European Union members, they can easily ignore the troubled inhabitants. Cyprus has always been strategically important for the various tyrannical old Empires; hence the reason why Cyprus was colonized for more than two and a half thousand years.

Cyprus is an island situated in the north-east corner of the Mediterranean, with Turkey to the north, Syria to the east and 480 miles southeast of mainland Greece. Its maximum length, from Cape Arnauti in the west to Cape Andreas at the end of the north-eastern peninsula, is 140 miles; the maximum north-south extent is 60 miles. With an area of 3,572 square miles (9,251 square kilometres), it is the third largest Mediterranean island (after Sicily and Sardinia). The general pattern of its 486-mile coastline is indented and rocky, with long, sandy beaches.

The Kyrenia coast on the north has a range of steep limestone mountains along most of its length. South of that is a treeless plain, hot and arid in summer, while further south still are igneous mountains rising to 1,950 m (6,400 feet). Here seasonally heavy rainfall has caused erosion, for winter torrents rush down unchecked. Lack of consistent rainfall is ameliorated by a high water-table which allows the use of wells.

In the south, exports of manufactured goods such as clothing, and agricultural products, together with the successful development of tourism, contribute to a thriving economy. Vineyards and orchards flourish, and sheep and goats graze the hills. Cyprus (Greek, 'copper') still has some copper, as well as iron pyrites and asbestos. The north, by contrast, is primarily agricultural and is dependent on Turkish aid.

2. SHORT HISTORY OF CYPRUS

CYPRUS BEFORE THE SEPARATION

A Mycenaean colony in the 14th century BC, it was ruled successively by the Assyrian, Persian, Roman, and Byzantine empires. Richard I of England conquered it in 1191 and sold it to the French Crusader Guy de Lusignan under whom it became a feudal monarchy. An important base for the Crusades, it eventually came under the control of Italian trading states, until in 1571 it fell to the Ottoman Empire. It remained part of the Ottoman Empire until 1879, when it was placed under British administration.

It was formally annexed by Britain in 1914 and in 1925 declared a crown colony. From the outset there was rivalry between Greek- and Turkish-speaking communities, the former, the majority, desiring union (*enosis*) with Greece. After World War II there was much civil violence in which the Greek Cypriot terrorist organization EOKA played the leading role.

In 1960 independence within the Commonwealth was granted under the presidency of Archbishop Makarios, but by 1964 the government was in chaos and a United Nations peace-keeping force intervened.

In 1974 a Greek Cypriot coup overthrew the president and Turkish forces invaded, gaining virtual control over most of the island. The Greek national government which had backed the revolt, collapsed. Talks in Geneva between Britain, Turkey, Greece, and the two Cypriot communities failed, and, although Makarios was able to resume the presidency in 1975, the Turkish Federated State of

Cyprus was formed in northern Cyprus, comprising some 38 per cent of the island, with its own president.

In 1983 it proclaimed itself the Turkish Republic of Northern Cyprus. Britain retained an important RAF base, which was also a key intelligence centre. In the early 1990s the presidents of the two communities held talks on uniting the island, but no agreement was reached.

First Settlement

The first human settlement was in the Neolithic period, at a date now calculated as well before 6500 BC. The immigration of settlers from Greece, which began in about 1200 BC, led to the foundation of Greek kingdoms covering almost the whole of the island and to the dominance of the Greek language.

Since then, Cyprus has come under the influence or control of the various peoples that have exercised power in the eastern Mediterranean--Phoenicians, Assyrians, Babylonians, Egyptians, Persians, the Greek monarchies of Alexander the Great and his successors, the Roman Empire from its successive capitals of Rome and Constantinople, French crusaders, Genoese, Venetians, Turks, and, more recently, the British.

British Occupation

Britain maintains two military bases, at Akrotiri and Dhekelia, in the south of the island. They have a combined area of 99 square miles. The British occupation began in 1878 and ended in August 1960, when Cyprus became independent as the Republic of Cyprus (Greek Kipriakí Demokratía, Turkish Kbrs Cumhuriyeti), with its capital at Nicosia.

The long-standing conflict between the Greek-Cypriot majority and the Turkish-Cypriot minority intensified; in 1974 an invasion by Turkish troops produced an effective although unrecognized partition of the island and led to the declaration in 1975 of a separate Turkish-Cypriot state in the northern part. The Turkish-Cypriot state made a unilateral declaration of independence in 1983 and adopted the name Turkish Republic of Northern Cyprus. Its independence was recognized only by Turkey.

3. REPUBLIC OF CYPRUS

CYPRIOT FLAG

The first general election took place on July 31, 1960. Of the 35 seats allotted to the Greek Cypriots, 30 were won by supporters of Makarios, 5 by agreement being allotted to the Communist-led Progressive Party of the Working People (AKEL). All 15 Turkish-Cypriot seats were won by supporters of Küçük Mehmet. The republic came into being on Aug. 16, 1960, and Cyprus was admitted as a member of the United Nations. The British government agreed to pay 12,000,000 in financial assistance over five years. Cyprus was admitted to membership in the Commonwealth in March 1961.

The difficulties experienced in implementing some of the complicated provisions of the constitution, particularly over local government and finance, led Makarios late in 1963 to propose to Küçük 13 amendments. These were rejected by the Turkish government and the Turkish Cypriots, and in the next month

7

fighting broke out between the two Cypriot communities. As a result, the area controlled by the Turkish Cypriots was reduced to a few enclaves, and Nicosia was divided by a cease-fire line, policed to begin with by British troops. In March 1964 the UN Security Council agreed to send to Cyprus a multinational force known as the United Nations Peace-Keeping Force in Cyprus, or UNFICYP.

Its mandate was extended repeatedly in the course of the continuing conflict. In 1964 intensified fighting in the northwest caused the Turkish air force to intervene; at the same time a full-scale invasion was threatened. Contingents of troops from Greece and Turkey were brought into the island clandestinely together with officers to command and train the forces raised by the two communities. Grivas, who had been promoted to lieutenant general in the Greek army, returned from Greece to command the Greek-Cypriot National Guard.

In 1967 an incident in the southeast led to a Turkish ultimatum to Greece, backed by the threat of invasion. The military junta then ruling Greece complied by withdrawing the mainland contingents together with General Grivas. An uneasy peace was established, but inter-communal talks failed to produce a solution.

Makarios was re-elected president in 1968 by an overwhelming majority, and in 1973 his re-election was not even contested. Although Makarios had originally been a leader in the campaign for enosis, he was thought by many Greek Cypriots and mainland Greeks to be content with Cyprus' independence after he became president. Dissidents angered by that perception are assumed to have tried to assassinate him in 1970 and 1973. In 1973 Makarios was denounced by the three suffragan bishops ecclesiastically subordinate to him; they demanded that he renounce the presidency because it was in conflict with his role as a spiritual leader.

Makarios circumvented them, however, by calling a synod of the Eastern Orthodox churches presided over by the Patriarch of Alexandria. Meanwhile Grivas had returned secretly to Cyprus in 1971 to resume the campaign for enosis under a newly formed EOKA-B; he died in Limassol in 1974, at the age of 75.

Economy after Independence

Between 1960 and 1973 the Republic of Cyprus, operating a free enterprise economy based on agriculture and trade, achieved a standard of living higher than most of its neighbours, with the exception of Israel. This progress was substantially assisted by various agencies of the United Nations, operating through the UN Development Program.

Generous financial assistance was given by the World Bank and the International Monetary Fund in the form of loans for specific development projects (electricity supply, port development, and sewerage, among others). Aid was also made available by individual foreign countries.

Experts were provided to advise on economic planning and to initiate productive projects, and training for Cypriot specialists was encouraged by scholarships and grants. During this period the gross domestic product grew at an average annual rate of over 7 percent, and per capita national income by about 6 percent annually. Agricultural production doubled; industrial production and exports of goods and services more than trebled. Tourism became the largest single earner of foreign exchange.

Nicosia, the Capital

Greek LEVKOSÍA, Turkish LEFKO<u>S</u>A, city and capital of the Republic of Cyprus. It lies along the Pedieos River, in the centre of the Mesaoria Plain between the Kyrenia Mountains (north) and the Troodos range (south). The city is also the archiepiscopal seat of the autocephalous (having the right to elect its own archbishop and bishops) Church of Cyprus.

Nicosia came successively under the control of the Byzantines (330-1191), the Lusignan kings (1192-1489), the Venetians (1489-1571), the Turks (1571-1878), and the British (1878-1960), and thus reflects the vicissitudes of Cypriot history and both Eastern and Western influences. Nicosia, known in antiquity as Ledra, is a medieval corruption of the Byzantine name Lefkosia.

The city was a kingdom in the 7th century BC and has been a bishopric from the 4th century AD. It has been the seat of government of Cyprus since the 10th century. The city's walled

9

fortifications, originally erected by the Lusignan kings and later rebuilt by the Venetians to encompass a smaller area (3 miles [5 km] round), did not prevent invasions by the Genoese in 1373, the Mamluks in 1426, and the Turks in 1570.

Standing in mute testimony to the religious and political changes of the city is the Cathedral of St. Sophia. Begun in 1209, completed in 1325, and pillaged by invaders, it was converted into the chief mosque of Cyprus in 1571. Its name was changed to the Selimiye Mosque in honour of the Ottoman sultan Selim II, under whose reign Cyprus was conquered.

During the 20th century the city boundaries were extended beyond the existing circular Venetian walls, and the old town within them was rebuilt. As a result of the Turkish intervention in 1974, part of the northern section of Nicosia, including the former international airport, has remained within the United Nations Forces in Cyprus operational boundary separating the Republic of Cyprus (south) from the Turkish Cypriot administered areas (north). The city also experienced an influx of an estimated 35,000 Greek Cypriot refugees from the north in the mid-1970s.

Nicosia's light industries, mainly serving the local market, include the manufacture and processing of cotton yarns and textiles, cigarettes, flour, confectionery, soft drinks, footwear, and clothing. Nicosia is connected by good roads with the other major towns of the island; a new international airport was established in 1974 at Larnaca, about 21 miles (34 km) southeast of Nicosia.

The Cyprus Museum in the city houses many archaeological treasures. Most of the population in the surrounding area is engaged in agriculture, and crops produced include wheat, barley, vegetables, and fruits; goats and sheep are also raised. Pop. (1988 est.) city, incl. suburbs, 166,900.

Pedieos River

Also spelled as PEDIEAS, Greek PEDIAÍOS, Turkish PEDIYAS, this is the river in central and eastern Cyprus. It rises in the Troodos range and flows in a north-easterly direction toward Nicosia, where it takes an easterly turn through the part of the central lowlands called the Mesaoria Plain toward Famagusta Bay.

Although the longest (about 60 miles [100 km]) in Cyprus, the river is not navigable. Formerly emptying into the bay near the ancient city of Salamis, it now drains into irrigation reservoirs near Akhyritou and Kouklia, west of Famagusta.

Limassol

APHRODITE BEACH NEAR LIMASSOL

In Greek this city is called LEMESÓS, in Turkish LIMASOL. It is the chief port of the Republic of Cyprus. The city lies on Akrotiri Bay, on the southern coast, southwest of Nicosia; it is the island's second largest city and is also its chief tourist centre.

Limassol's rise from a humble market town between the ancient settlements of Amathus and Curium took place at the end of the Byzantine Empire, when Richard I the Lion-Heart landed there in 1191 and was married to Berengaria of Navarre in the chapel of a castle fortress, now a regional museum and one of only two surviving buildings of the period.

After the Genoese seizure of Famagusta in 1372, the port's fortunes increased; but damage from numerous incursions between 1414 and 1426, the Turkish invasion of 1570, and a disastrous earthquake had reduced its population to 150 by 1815. Its resurgence dates from the end of the 19th century, when the island came under British administration.

Limassol's harbour facilities, which were extended in the 1960s to improve its shallow-water location, were increased by a new port (operational in 1974) that was able to provide berthing spaces for large vessels. The Turkish intervention (1974) in northern Cyprus and the closing of the island's main port at Famagusta made Limassol the chief port of the Republic of Cyprus.

The port has also taken over much of the trade that once passed through Beirut. In the 1970s and '80s Limassol also became home to many thousands of prosperous Arab refugees from Lebanon and immigrants from Saudi Arabia and Kuwait. Limassol's bustling port exports wines, beverages, fruits, and vegetables.

Bricks, tiles, shoes, textiles, furniture, cement, buttons, and soft drinks are manufactured; fruit is canned; and chrome and asbestos are processed. Legumes, vegetables, oranges, lemons, grapefruits, nuts, and apples are grown on the adjacent coastal plain, and goats and cattle are raised as well.

The Troodos Mountains lie inland from the plain. Limassol city is linked by roads with Moni, Akrotíri, and Episkopi. Pop. (1982) city, 74,782; (1989 est.) metropolitan area, 120,000.

Paphos

PAPHOS HARBOUR

Called PÁFOS in Greek, the town is in the south-western section of the Republic of Cyprus. Paphos was also the name of two ancient cities that were the precursors of the modern town. The older ancient city (Greek: Palia Paphos) was located at modern Pírgos (Kouklia); New Paphos, which had superseded Old Paphos by Roman times, was 10 miles (16 km) farther west. New Paphos and Ktima together form modern Paphos.

Old Paphos, which was settled by Greek colonists in the Mycenaean period, contained a famous temple of Aphrodite and was the legendary site where Aphrodite was born from the sea foam. In Hellenic times Paphos was second only to Salamis in extent and influence among the states of Cyprus.

KINGS' TOMBS IN PAPHOS

The Cinyrad dynasty ruled Paphos until its final conquest by Ptolemy I of Egypt (294 BC). Old Paphos dwindled in influence after the fall of the Cinyradae, the foundation of New Paphos, and the Roman conquest of Cyprus (58 BC). It was finally deserted after the 4th century AD.

New Paphos, which had been the port town of Old Paphos, became the administrative capital of the whole island in Ptolemaic and Roman times. The city was attacked and destroyed by Muslim raiders in AD 960. The modern town began to grow only after the

British occupation in 1878. The harbour, centre of the city's life, was improved in 1908 and 1959 but remains too small to handle large commercial traffic and thus serves only an active local fishing fleet.

Despite economic difficulties arising from the settlement in Paphos of some 5,000 Greek Cypriot refugees after the Turkish occupation of 1974, by the end of the decade the city had become the focus of strong economic development, including an industrial estate and tourist hotels.

The city's manufacturing consists of small enterprises producing clothing, footwear, canned meat, beverages, and vegetable oils. Local points of interest include Orthodox churches, the Djami Kebir Mosque, Paphos Castle, and Frankish baths. Pop. (1982 est.) 13,100.

Cultural Life

The very ancient cultural traditions of Cyprus are maintained partly by private enterprise and partly by government activity, especially on the part of the Cultural Service of the Republic of Cyprus' Ministry of Education.

The Cultural Service publishes books and awards prizes for literature. Mobile libraries operate in rural areas. The government-sponsored Cyprus Theatrical Organization stages plays by contemporary Cypriot dramatists as well as classical works. The ancient theatres of Salamis, Curium, and Soli have been restored and are used for the staging of a variety of plays, and a Greek theatre has been built at Nicosia.

Many painters and sculptors work in Cyprus, and the Cultural Service keeps the state's collection of modern Cypriot art on permanent exhibition. In the village of Lemba near Paphos the Cyprus College of Art runs courses for postgraduate art students. Government encouragement is given to young composers.

Television and radio are controlled by the semi-governmental Cyprus Broadcasting Corporation and are financed by advertising. The Turkish sector receives broadcasts from Turkey. Languages used are Greek, Turkish, English, and Armenian. Many daily and weekly newspapers are published in Greek, Turkish, and English.

Local Government

Local government in the Republic of Cyprus is at the district, municipal, rural municipality, and village level. District officers are appointed by the government; local councils are elected, as are the mayors of municipalities.

Justice

The legal code of Cyprus is based on Roman law. In the Greek-Cypriot zone judges are appointed by the government, but the judiciary is entirely independent of the executive power. There are a supreme court and an appeals court, district assize courts handling criminal matters, and district courts exercising summary jurisdiction. The Turkish-Cypriot zone has a similar system of justice.

Political parties

The oldest established political party in the Republic of Cyprus is the Anorthotiko Komma Ergazomenou Laou (AKEL; Progressive Party of the Working People), founded in 1941. It is a pro-Moscow Communist party, and it controls the principal trade union federation; its share of the vote in the first 50 years of the Republic of Cyprus was usually in the neighbourhood of 30 percent.

Other parties have had varying success. Among them are the Eniea Demokratiki Enosis Kyprou (Cyprus National Democratic Union), a Socialist party; the Enosi Kentrou (Centre Union); the Demokratikos Synagermos (Democratic Rally); and the Demokratiko Komma (Democratic Party).

In the Turkish-Cypriot zone the major parties are the Ulusal Birlik Partisi (National Unity Party) and the Toplumcu Kurtulus Partisi (Communal Liberation Party).

Industry

Resources of raw materials on Cyprus are very limited, restricting the scope for industrial activity. Before the partition of the island most manufacturing was of goods produced for the domestic market by small, owner-operated plants, and a considerable number of those plants were located in the area that was occupied by the Turks in 1974.

Industries in the Republic of Cyprus were subsequently reoriented toward production for export, and a number of larger factories were built in the south. Petroleum refining, cement and asbestos pipe production, and thermal electricity production are the republic's heavy industries, and its light industries produce goods such as clothing, footwear, and machinery and transport equipment.

Tourism became one of Cyprus' major industries after 1960. About 65 percent of tourist accommodation, however, was in the portion of the island that was occupied by the Turks in 1974. After partition the tourist trade recovered rapidly in the Greek-Cypriot sector: to counter the loss of Kyrenia and the Famagusta-Varosha area, which had been the leading seaside resorts, the southern coastal towns of Limassol, Larnaca, and Paphos were further developed to accommodate tourists.

Ethnic composition

The people of Cyprus represent two main ethnic groups, Greek and Turkish. The Greek Cypriots, who constitute the majority, are descended from a mixture of aboriginal inhabitants with immigrants from the Peloponnese who colonized Cyprus about 1100 BC and assimilated subsequent settlers up to the 16th century.

The Turkish Cypriots are the descendants of the soldiers of the Ottoman army that conquered the island in 1571 and of immigrants from Anatolia brought in by the Sultan's government shortly thereafter. Since 1974 additional immigrants from Anatolia, with their families, have been brought in to work vacant land and increase the total labour force.

Linguistic composition

The language of the majority is Greek and of the minority Turkish. English is widely spoken and understood as a second language. Illiteracy is low, thanks to the excellence of the educational system.

Finance and trade

The Republic of Cyprus began to expand financial services, including offshore banking, in 1982. Light manufactures particularly clothing and footwear, and foodstuffs, including potatoes and citrus fruit, constitute the Republic of Cyprus' major exports. Machinery and transport equipment, petroleum and petroleum products, and foodstuffs and live animals are imported.

Chronic trade deficits are offset by receipts from tourists, remittances sent home by expatriate Greek Cypriots and receipts from the British military bases on the island. In the Turkish sector, citrus fruits, potatoes, and carobs are the principal exports.

Transportation

In Roman times the island had a well-developed road system, but by the time of the British occupation in 1878 the only carriage road was between Nicosia and Larnaca. An extensive new road network was built under the British administration. A narrow-gauge public railway proved uneconomical and was closed in the early 1950s. Because there are no public railways, inland travel depends entirely upon roads, and motor transport has greatly increased.

International air services provide connections to all parts of Europe and the Middle East and to some points in Africa. Nicosia International Airport was closed in 1974 and the airport at Larnaca was developed in its stead. An airport at Paphos, opened in 1985, is also used for international flights. An airport at Gecitiikale (Lefkoniko) in the Turkish-occupied sector is used by flights coming from or through Turkey.

There is no coastal shipping, and much of the merchant marine registered to Cyprus is foreign-owned. The great bulk of the island's international trade remains seaborne, however, the main ports being Limassol and Larnaca; Turkish shipping uses Famagusta.

Government and social conditions

The constitution of the Republic of Cyprus, adopted in 1960, provided that the executive power be exercised by a Greek-Cypriot president and a Turkish-Cypriot vice president, elected to five-year terms by universal suffrage, and that there be a Council of Ministers (Cabinet) comprising seven Greek-Cypriot and three Turkish-Cypriot members. There was also to be an elected House of Representatives with 50 seats, divided between Greek and Turkish Cypriots in the proportion of 35 to 15 and elected for five years.

The constitution, derived from the negotiations in Zürich in 1959 between representatives of the governments of Greece and Turkey, did not inspire enthusiasm among the citizens of the new republic, however.

The Greek Cypriots, whose struggle against the British had been for enosis (union with Greece) and not for independence, regretted the failure to achieve this national aspiration. As a result it was not long after the establishment of the republic before the Greek-Cypriot majority began to regard many of the provisions, particularly those relating to finance and to local government, as unworkable.

Proposals for amendment were rejected by the Turkish government and, after the outbreak of fighting between the two Cypriot communities in late 1963; the constitution went largely into abeyance.

In the territory controlled by the government of the Republic of Cyprus after the Turkish occupation of 1974, the constitution's provisions are considered as still in force where practicable; the main formal change has been the gradual increase of the number of seats in the House of Representatives, all of which are held by Greek Cypriots.

On the Turkish side of the demarcation line there have been, since 1974, an elected president, prime minister, and legislative assembly, all serving five-year terms of office. A new constitution was approved for the Turkish Republic of Northern Cyprus by its electorate in 1985.

Land of Cyprus

The saucepan shape of Cyprus results from its topography, which, in turn, reflects its geology. The 100-mile-long Kyrenia Mountains-- the western portion of which also is known as the Pentadactylos for the five-fingered peak that is one of the range's main features--runs parallel to and just inland from the northern coast. It is the southernmost range of the great Alpine-Himalayan chain in the eastern Mediterranean; like much of that extensive mountain belt it is formed largely of thrust masses of Mesozoic limestone.

The Troodos Mountains in the south and southwest are of great interest to geologists, who have concluded that the range, made up of igneous rock, was formed from molten rock beneath the deep ocean (Tethys) that once separated the continents of Eurasia and Afro-Arabia. The range stretches eastward about 50 miles from near the island's west coast to Stavrovouni peak (2,260 feet [689 metres]), about 12 miles from the southeast coast. The range's summit, Mt. Olympus (also called Mt. Troodos), reaches an altitude of 6,401 feet (1,951 metres).

Kyrenia Mountains

This mountain range in northern Cyprus extends east to west for about 100 miles (160 km) from Cape Andreas, on the Karpas Peninsula, to Cape Kormakiti. Rising from the coast a short distance inland, the range flanks a narrow coastal plain and reaches a maximum height of 3,360 feet (1,024 m) at Mount Kyparissovouno, in the western region, ending in low hills at the tip of Cape Andreas in the east.

West of Melounda, the range is known as the Pentadaktylos ("Five Fingers"), from the fingered peak that is one of its main features. The first area extensively settled by mainland Turks after the Turkish intervention in Cyprus in 1974 stretches from the eastern part of Ayios Amvrosios to the Karpass Peninsula and across the Pentadaktylos mountains. The mountains are composed of a narrow fold of limestone with occasional deposits of marble.

Between the two ranges lies the Mesaoria Plain (its name means "Between the Mountains"). The plain, which is flat and low-lying, extends from Morphou Bay in the west to Famagusta Bay in the east. Roughly in the centre of the plain is the capital, Nicosia (Greek Levkosía; Turkish Lefkoṣa). The plain is the principal cereal-growing area in the island. About half of its 465,500 acres are irrigated; the remainder are devoted to dryland farming.

Drainage

All of the major rivers in Cyprus originate in the Troodos Mountains. The Pedieos, which is the largest, flows eastward toward Famagusta Bay; the Karyoti flows westward to Morphou Bay; and the Kouris flows southward to Episkopi Bay. The rivers are dependent on winter rainfall; in summer they become dry courses.

Plant and animal life

There is a narrow fertile plain along the northern coast where the vegetation is largely evergreen but also includes olive, carob, and citrus trees. The Troodos range has a covering of pine, dwarf oak, cypress, and cedar forest. The southern and western slopes are extensively planted with vines.

Between autumn and spring the Mesaoria Plain is green and colourful, with an abundance of wildflowers and flowering bushes and shrubs; there are also patches of woodland in which eucalyptus and many types of acacia, cypress, and lowland pine are found. At the island's western end in the area around Morphou there are orange plantations.

Fossil remains of elephant and hippopotamus have been found in the Kyrenia area, and in classical times there were large numbers of deer and boar, but the only large wild animal now surviving is the *agrino*, a species of wild sheep related to the mouflon of the western Mediterranean. It is under strict protection in a small forested area of the Troodos range. Small game is abundant but keenly hunted. Snakes, in classical times so ubiquitous as to earn the island the name of Ophiussa, "the Abode of Snakes," are now comparatively rare.

Cyprus lies on major migration routes for birds and in spring and autumn many millions pass through. Many species also winter on the island. There are many resident species, including francolin and chukar partridges.

Climate

Cyprus has an intense Mediterranean climate with a typically strongly marked seasonal rhythm. Hot dry summers from June to September and rainy, rather changeable, winters from November to March are separated by short autumn and spring seasons of rapid change in October and in April and May. Autumn and winter rain, on which agriculture and water supply in general depend, is variable.

Average annual rainfall is about 20 inches (500 millimetres). The lowest average precipitation is 14 inches at Nicosia and the highest 41 inches on Mt. Olympus. At Nicosia summer temperatures range between an average daily maximum of 98° F (37° C) and an average daily minimum of 70° F (21° C); in winter the range is between 59° F (15° C) and 41° F (5° C). From December to March the Troodos range experiences several weeks of below-freezing night temperatures.

Resources

Cyprus was for many centuries a noted producer of copper; in Greek the name of the island and the name of the metal are identical. As early as 2500 BC its mines were being exploited, and traces of prehistoric and Roman workings and surface slags are still to be seen. With the discovery of other sources the mines remained neglected for many centuries until they were reopened shortly before World War I. They were exploited more seriously from 1925 until they were closed by the Great Depression of the 1930s.

After World War II they were brought back into production, and since then copper and other minerals--iron pyrites, asbestos, gypsum, and chrome ore--have contributed moderately to the export trade. Reserves of copper ore have declined but there are substantial reserves of asbestos, chrome, gypsum, and iron pyrites. There are also extensive quarries of good building stone. The island's most important copper mines are located in the area of Skouriotissa in the Turkish-occupied zone.

Religions

The Greek Cypriots are Eastern Orthodox Christians. Their church, the Church of Cyprus, is autocephalous--*i.e.*, not under the authority of any patriarch; this privilege was granted to Archbishop Anthemius in AD 488 by the Byzantine emperor Zeno.

Under the Ottoman Empire the archbishop of the Church of Cyprus was made responsible for the secular as well as the religious behaviour of the Orthodox community and given the title ethnarch.

The Turkish Cypriots are Sunni Muslims. There are also Maronites, Armenians, Roman Catholics, and Anglicans on the island.

Demographic trends

Cypriots at times have emigrated in large numbers and it is estimated that as many live abroad as on the island itself. The great majority of emigrants have always gone to the United Kingdom and the rest mainly to the English-speaking countries: Australia, South Africa, the United States, and Canada.

Waves of heavy emigration followed the negotiation of independence in 1960 and the Turkish invasion in 1974. As a result of emigration and other factors, such as war losses and a temporary decline in fertility, the population decreased by about 5 percent between mid-1974 and 1977. The years since 1974 also have been marked by an increase in persons leaving the island in search of work, especially in the Middle East.

Education

Six grades of free and compulsory elementary education are provided for children beginning at age six. At least three years of the six-year secondary education program are free, and all secondary education at technical schools is free. Post-secondary facilities include schools for teacher training, technical instruction, hotel and catering training, nursing, and midwifery. Recent university education offers graduate and post-graduate degrees in many art and science subjects.

The education system in the Turkish sector is administered separately. Although Cyprus has a few new universities, many students attend universities abroad, especially in Greece, Turkey, Britain, or the United States.

Health

Health standards are high because of a favourable climate and well-organized public and private health services. Since the eradication of malaria shortly after World War II and, later, of echinococcosis (hydatid disease), the island has been free from major diseases.

Agriculture, forestry, and fishing

Of the arable land on the island, about one-fourth is irrigated, mainly in the Mesaoria Plain and around Paphos in the southwest. Pastures occupy about 10 percent of the total land area. Landholdings are generally small, highly fragmented, and dispersed under traditional laws of inheritance. A program of land consolidation was enacted in 1969, but it met with resistance, particularly from Turkish-Cypriot landowners, and was only very slowly implemented.

The major crops of the Greek-Cypriot sector include grapes, deciduous fruits, vegetables, olives, and carobs. The area under Turkish occupation produces the bulk of the country's citrus fruits, wheat, barley, carrots, tobacco, and green fodder.

Livestock--especially sheep, goats, and pigs--and livestock products historically have accounted for about one-third of the island's total agricultural production. Some cattle are also raised.

Cyprus was once famous for its extensive forests, but the demand for timber for shipbuilding by successive conquerors from the 7th century BC onward, and extensive felling for building and for fuel, has destroyed the greater part.

Under the British administration a vigorous policy of conservation and reforestation was pursued, and the Cyprus Forestry College was established at Prodhromos, on the western slopes of Mt. Olympus. Forests cover some 520 square miles, most of them being found in the mountain areas and in the Paphos district.

The fishing industry is small, in part because coastal waters are deficient in nutrients and associated plankton. Although the industry has shown some growth in the Greek-Cypriot sector, most fish is imported.

4. MODERN HISTORICAL INFLUENTIAL NAMES

Makarios III.

(Born August. 13, 1913, in Pano Panayia, Paphos, and died August 3, 1977, in Nicosia.)

His original name was **MIKHAIL KHRISTODOULOU MOUSKOS.** As church tradition has it, when he was chosen as archbishop and primate of the Orthodox Church of Cyprus, he adopted the name of Makarios. He was a leader in the struggle for enosis (union) with Greece during the post-war British occupation, and, from 1959 until his death in 1977, he was the president of independent Cyprus.

The son of a poor shepherd, Mouskos studied in Cyprus and at the University of Athens and later at the School of Theology of Boston University. He was ordained in 1946, became bishop of Kition (Larnaca) in 1948, and on October 18, 1950, was made archbishop.

During that time Makarios became identified with the movement for enosis, the archbishop of Cyprus having traditionally played an important political role during the Turkish occupation as ethnarch, or head of the Greek Christian community. Opposing the British government's proposals for independence or Commonwealth status, as well as Turkish pressures for partition in order to safeguard the island's sizable Turkish population, Makarios met with the Greek prime minister, Alexandros Papagos, in February 1954 and gained Greek support for enosis.

He was soon suspected by the British of being a leading figure in Colonel Georgios Grivas' terrorist organization. Makarios, however, preferred political bargaining to force, negotiating with the British governor in 1955-56. When these talks proved fruitless and Makarios was arrested for sedition in March 1956 and exiled, the guerrillas began a reign of terror. In February 1959 Makarios accepted a compromise that resulted in independence for Cyprus. He was elected president of the new republic on Dec. 13, 1959, with a Turkish vice president.

Makarios' administration was marred by fighting between Greeks and Turks, particularly after December 1963, and the active intervention of both Greece and Turkey. Previously a champion of exclusively Greek interests, he now worked for integration of the two communities, measures the Turks repeatedly resisted.

In December 1967 he was obliged to accept a Turkish Cypriot Provisional Administration, which managed Turkish minority affairs outside the jurisdiction of the central government. Despite communal strife, he was elected president for a second term in February 1968. Talks between the two communities remained deadlocked over the question of local autonomy. In 1972 and 1973 other Cypriot bishops called for Makarios to resign, but he was returned unopposed for a third term as head of state in 1973.

In July 1974 the Greek Cypriot National Guard, whose officers were mainland Greeks, attempted a coup, planned by the ruling military junta in Athens, to achieve enosis. Makarios fled to Malta and then to London and Turkey invaded Cyprus and proclaimed a separate state for Turkish Cypriots in the north. Makarios. vowing to resist partition of the island, returned to Cyprus in December, after the fall of the mainland Greek military junta.

Grivas, Georgios (Theodoros)

(Born May 23, 1898, in Trikomo and died on January 27, 1974 in Limassol.)

Grivas was also called DIGHENIS, the Cypriot patriot who helped bring Cyprus independence in 1960. His goal was enosis (union) with Greece, and in this he failed; indeed, he was a fugitive at the time of his death.

Grivas organized EOKA (Ethnikí Orgánosis Kipriakoú Agónos, or National Organization of Cypriot Struggle) about 1955, after leading a right-wing resistance group in the Athens area during the German occupation of World War II. With his friend, afterward his enemy, the Orthodox cleric Makarios III, Grivas conducted a guerrilla war against the British that led to the independence of Cyprus but not to the enosis that was always his objective. After a period of retirement in Greece, Grivas returned to Cyprus in 1971 to revitalize the underground movement against Makarios (then president of Cyprus). On his death, his followers vowed to continue his terrorist campaign for enosis.

EOKA

This is the abbreviation OF ETHNIKÍ ORGÁNOSIS KIPRIAKOÚ AGÓNOS (Greek: "National Organization of Cypriot Struggle"), the underground nationalist movement of Greek Cypriots dedicated to the expulsion of the British from Cyprus (achieved in 1960) and the eventual union (Greek *énosis*) of Cyprus with Greece.

EOKA was organized *c.* 1955 by Col. Georgios Grivas, an officer in the Greek Army, with the support of Makarios III, Orthodox archbishop of Cyprus. Its patriotic campaign, begun early in 1955, reached a climax in 1956, with the exile of Makarios and the temporary depletion of British forces in the island because of the Suez crisis.

By early 1957, however, a reinforced British army successfully attacked the terrorists' mountain hideouts, considerably weakening EOKA, which had never numbered more than 300 men. Violence subsided after Makarios' release in March 1957, though there was a recurrence in mid-1958, when EOKA clashed with Turkish Cypriot guerrillas. In 1958 Makarios announced he would accept independence for Cyprus rather than *énosis*, and in March 1959 Grivas reluctantly disbanded his organization after obtaining amnesty for its members.

In 1971 Grivas, who had served for a time as commander of the Greek Cypriot National Guard but had been recalled by the Greek government, re-entered Cyprus secretly to form EOKA B, to "prevent a betrayal of *énosis*." After Grivas' death in January 1974, his followers vowed to continue the struggle. President Makarios officially proscribed EOKA B in April 1974, three months before he was ousted and before Turkish forces landed and divided the country in a brief civil war.

Thereafter, EOKA disappeared, but it is said that the few remaining members of EOKA B are still ultra-right wing nationalists (to the point of being considered neo-Nazis) who still maintain that Cyprus should unite with Greece, the same way as Rhodes, Crete and other islands did.

5. PREHISTORIC AND RECENT EVENTS

Human habitation

The earliest evidence of human habitation on Cyprus comes from the Neolithic Period. The settlement at Khirokitia (near the southern coast), which is now dated to well before 6500 BC, is one of the most remarkable Neolithic communities ever excavated in Europe. It was a town of about 2,000 inhabitants, living in well-built round stone houses of two stories. The Khirokitians made little use of pottery, using stone and presumably wood, for utensils and stone for tools.

The presence of flakes of obsidian, which is not native to the non-volcanic island of Cyprus, is the only sign of contact with other cultures. Khirokitia and a few smaller associated settlements appear to have died out after a few centuries, leaving the island uninhabited again for some 2,000 years.

The remains of the Neolithic settlement at Khirokitia were designated a UNESCO World Heritage site.

The beginning of the next period of habitation, known as the Sotira culture, is dated to between 4500 and 4000 BC; small villages of this culture are found not only at Sotira (near the southern coast, north of Curium) but also in the Kyrenia range. Small ornaments of picrolite (a variety of soapstone) and a progressively more attractive pottery distinguish the Sotira culture; toward the end of the period copper came into use.

Turkish invasion

On July 15, 1974, a detachment of the National Guard, led by officers from mainland Greece, launched a coup aimed at assassinating Makarios and establishing enosis. They laid the presidential palace in ruins, but Makarios narrowly escaped. A former EOKA member, Nikos Sampson (also owner of the nationalist newspaper Machi), was proclaimed president of Cyprus.

Five days later Turkish forces landed at Kyrenia with the expressed aim of overturning Sampson's government. Vigorous resistance was offered, but the Turks were successful in establishing a bridgehead around Kyrenia and linking it with the Turkish sector of Nicosia.

On July 23 Greece's junta fell and was replaced by a democratic government under Konstantinos Karamanlis. At the same time, Sampson was replaced in Cyprus by Glafkos Clerides, who as president of the House of Representatives automatically succeeded the head of state in the latter's absence.

The three guarantor powers, Britain, Greece, and Turkey, as required by the treaty, met for discussions in Geneva, but it proved impossible to halt the Turkish advance until August 16. By that time Turkey controlled the northern 37 percent of the island. In December Makarios returned to resume the presidency.

Effects of partition

The Turkish occupation of 37 percent of the country in 1974, involving the displacement of about a third of the population, dealt a serious blow to economic development. Losses of land and personal property in the occupied areas were very great. The gross domestic product of the Greek-Cypriot sector dropped sharply, the reduction amounting to 33 percent (at constant 1973 prices) between 1973 and 1975. By vigorous efforts real growth was resumed in the area left under the control of the government of the Republic of Cyprus, and between 1975 and 1983 the annual rate of growth was estimated to average about 8 percent.

The Turkish-occupied area did not enjoy the same prosperity, and its economy was supported by subsidies from the Turkish government. Trade between the two areas ceased and the two economies became entirely independent, although the southern zone continued to supply the northern with certain services such as electricity and the northern zone supplied water to the south.

Declaration of a Turkish state

In May 1983 Denktash broke off the inter-communal talks, and in November he proclaimed the Turkish Republic of Northern Cyprus (TRNC). The UN Security Council condemned the move and repeated its demand, first made in 1974, for the withdrawal of all foreign troops from the Republic of Cyprus. Renewed UN peace-proposal efforts in 1984 and 1985 were to no avail, however, and in

May 1985 a constitution for the TRNC was approved by referendum.

Inter-communal talks

Talks between Clerides and Rauf Denktash, representing the Greek and Turkish Cypriots, respectively, had begun in 1968. They continued inconclusively until 1974, the Turks demanding and the Greeks rejecting a bizonal federation with a weak central government. In February 1975 the Turkish Cypriots proclaimed the Turkish-occupied area the Turkish Federated State of Cyprus (a body calling itself the Provisional Cyprus-Turkish Administration had been in existence among Turkish Cypriots since 1967); Denktash announced that their purpose was not independence but federation.

Talks were resumed in Vienna in 1975 and 1976 under UN auspices. In early 1977 Makarios and Denktash agreed upon guidelines according to which Makarios could accept the principle of a bizonal federation.

In August 1977 Makarios died at the age of 64. Spyros Kyprianou, president of the House of Representatives, became acting president of the republic, and he was returned unopposed to that office for a five-year term in January 1978. An alliance between the President's Democratic Party and AKEL ensured Kyprianou's re-election as president in February 1983; Turkish Cypriots, however, took no part in the election.

Settlement patterns

The Cypriots were traditionally a largely rural people, but a steady drift to the towns began early in the 20th century. The census of 1973 recorded six towns, defined as settlements of more than 5,000 inhabitants, and almost 600 villages. This pattern was altered after the Turkish invasion of 1974 by the need to resettle in the southern part of the island some 180,000 Greek-Cypriot refugees from the Turkish-occupied north.

The accommodation built for them was situated mainly in the neighbourhood of the three towns south of the line of demarcation, and especially in the part of the Nicosia suburban area still controlled by the government of the Republic of Cyprus. In contrast, the northern portion of the island is now more thinly populated in spite of the influx of Turkish Cypriots transferred from the south and of immigrants from Turkey.

The six towns recorded in the 1973 census, under the undivided republic, were the headquarters of the island's six administrative districts. Of these Kyrenia (Turkish Girne), Famagusta (Greek Ammókhostos, Turkish Magusa), and the northern half of Nicosia are to the north of the demarcation line drawn in 1974 and are in Turkish-Cypriot hands.

Limassol, Larnaca, Paphos, and the southern part of Nicosia remained in Greek-Cypriot hands after 1974; the northern part of Nicosia became the administrative centre of the Turkish-Cypriot sector.

United Nations forces at the Green Line

The UN force in Cyprus observed its 35th anniversary in 1999 and could pride itself on having a generally favourable record in manning the Green Line, which divided the island between the Greek- and Turkish-Cypriot communities. Tensions continued during the year, but hostile incidents decreased. The Greek-Cypriot decision late in 1998 not to deploy a Russian-made air-defence missile system was generally welcomed. Border barriers were opened to allow visits by both Greek and Turkish Cypriots to religious shrines.

Negotiations for inclusion of the Republic of Cyprus in the European Union continued on schedule. The government endorsed the EU oil embargo of Yugoslavia but openly disagreed with the NATO bombings. Greek Cypriots generally supported the Orthodox Serbians in ways that ranged from demonstrations at the U.S. embassy to taking up collections to aid the Belgrade zoo. Turkish Cypriots supported the Muslim Kosovars. Rumours circulated that Kosovo refugees might be relocated to Turkish Cyprus, which added to the tension.

The economy, particularly on the Greek side, continued to be robust, if not booming. Foreign trade was slightly down, but tourism, mostly from Great Britain but with an increasingly important Russian contingent, was slightly up. Trade with Russia continued strong, with a volume of $400 million anticipated for

1999. Turkish Cyprus offset its trade deficit with revenue from tourists, about three-quarters of whom were from Turkey.

British rule

The Cyprus Convention of 1878 between Britain and Turkey provided that Cyprus, while remaining under Turkish sovereignty, should be administered by the British government. Britain's aim in occupying Cyprus was to secure a base in the eastern Mediterranean for possible operations in the Caucasus or Mesopotamia as part of the British guarantee to preserve the Sultan's Asian possessions from threat by Russia.

In 1914, however, Britain and Turkey being at war, the former proclaimed the island annexed; Turkish recognition was granted under the Treaty of Lausanne (1923), and the position was regularized in 1925 when Cyprus was declared a crown colony.

British occupation was initially welcomed by the Greek population, who from the start expected the British to transfer Cyprus to Greece. The Greek Cypriots' demand for enosis (union with Greece) and a corresponding hostility to it on the part of Turkish Cypriots constituted almost the sole division in politics; almost annual petitions demanding enosis were matched by counter-petitions and demonstrations from the Turkish Cypriots.

An offer to transfer the island had been made in 1915, on condition that Greece fulfil its treaty obligations toward Serbia when attacked by Bulgaria. The Greek government refused and the offer was not renewed. In 1931 the demand for enosis led to riots in Nicosia.

Cyprus was untouched by World War II apart from a few air raids. In 1947 the governor, in accordance with the British Labour Party's declaration on colonial policy, published proposals for greater self-government. They were rejected in favour of the slogan "enosis and only enosis."

Campaign for union

In 1955 Lieut. Col. Georgios Grivas (known as Dighenis), a Cypriot who had served as an officer in the Greek Army, began a concerted campaign for enosis. His National Organization of Cypriot Struggle (Ethnikí Orgánosis Kipriakoú Agónos; EOKA) bombed public

31

buildings and attacked and killed opponents of enosis, both Greek-Cypriot and British. Proposals for self-government were put forward at different times; the most advanced were those of the British jurist Lord Radcliffe in 1956.

All were rejected and the attacks continued. In March 1956 the archbishop, Makarios III, who as ethnarch considered it his duty to champion the national aspirations of the Greek Cypriots, was deported to the Seychelles. He was released from exile in March 1957 and left the Seychelles in April, but, being forbidden to return to Cyprus, he made his headquarters in Athens.

By this time the operations of EOKA were much reduced, but on the other hand the Turkish-Cypriot minority, led by Fazl Küçük, began to express alarm and demanded either retrocession to Turkey or partition. Public opinion in Greece and Turkey was much aroused in support of the two communities, resulting in riots and expulsions of Greek residents in Turkey. Frequent recourse to the United Nations produced no agreed solution.

The decisive step was taken by the Greek and Turkish governments, which in February 1959 reached agreement between themselves in Zürich. Later the same month, at a conference in London, the Greek-Turkish compromise was accepted by the British government and by representatives of the Greek-Cypriot and Turkish-Cypriot communities, led by Makarios and Küçük, respectively. In 1960 it was ratified by treaties agreed to in Nicosia.

Cyprus became an independent republic, with Britain retaining sovereignty over the two military bases at Akrotiri and Dhekélia. According to the terms of the treaties, the new republic would not participate in a political or economic union with any other state, nor would it be subject to partition. Greece, Turkey, and Britain guaranteed the independence, integrity, and security of the republic, and Greece and Turkey undertook to respect the integrity of the areas remaining under British sovereignty.

Makarios became president and Küçük vice president in elections held in December 1959. Decisions of the council of ministers would be binding on the president and vice president, either of whom could, however, exercise a veto in matters relating to security, defence, and foreign affairs. Turkish Cypriots, who made up less than 20 percent of the population, were to represent 30 percent of the civil service and 40 percent of the army and to elect one-third of the House of Representatives. A joint Greek and Turkish military headquarters was to be established.

Ottoman rule

A Turkish invading force landed in Cyprus in 1570 and captured Nicosia; the following year Famagusta fell after a long siege. Ottoman rule lasted more than three centuries. The Latin Church was suppressed and the Orthodox hierarchy restored; with the abolition of feudal tenure the Greek peasantry acquired inalienable and hereditary rights to land. Taxes were at first reduced but very soon were greatly increased and arbitrarily levied. In the 18th century the Orthodox archbishop was made responsible for tax collection.

About 20,000 Muslims (including the garrison, nominally 3,666 strong) were settled in the island in the immediate aftermath of the Ottoman conquest. Cyprus was an unimportant province to the sultans; its governors were slothful, inefficient, occasionally oppressive, and always venal. There were Turkish uprisings in 1764 and 1833; in 1821 the Orthodox archbishop was hanged on suspicion of sympathy with the rebellion in mainland Greece. The sultanate's various imperial proclamations in the 19th century promising reform had no effect in Cyprus, where local opposition prevented their application.

Battle of Lepanto

(Oct. 7, 1571)

This was the naval engagement between allied Christian forces and the Ottoman Turks during an Ottoman campaign to acquire the Venetian island of Cyprus. Seeking to drive Venice from the eastern Mediterranean, the forces of Sultan Selim II invaded Cyprus in 1570.

The Venetians formed an alliance with Pope Pius V and Philip II of Spain (May 25, 1571). Philip sent his half brother, Don John of Austria, to command the allied forces. By the time the allies assembled at Messina, Sicily (Aug. 24, 1571), the Turks had captured Nicosia (Sept. 9, 1570), besieged Famagusta, and entered the Adriatic. Their fleet lay in the Gulf of Patras, near Lepanto

(Návpaktos), Greece. The allied fleet of more than 200 ships sailed for Corfu on September 15 and on October 7 advanced in four squadrons against the Ottoman fleet, commanded by Ali Paşa, Muḥammad Saulak (governor of Alexandria), and Uluj Ali (dey of Algiers).

After about four hours of fighting, the allies were victorious, capturing 117 galleys and thousands of men. Of little practical value (Venice surrendered Cyprus to the Turks in 1573); the battle had a great impact on European morale and was the subject of paintings by Titian, Tintoretto, and Veronese.

Byzantine Empire

After the division of the Roman Empire (AD 395) Cyprus remained subject to the Eastern, or Byzantine, Empire at Constantinople, being part of the Diocese of the Orient governed from Antioch. In ecclesiastical matters, however, the Church of Cyprus was autocephalous--*i.e.*, independent of the Patriarchate of Antioch-- having been given that privilege in 488 by the emperor Zeno. The archbishop received the rights, still valued and practiced, of carrying a sceptre instead of a crozier and writing his signature in ink of imperial purple.

There was a break in direct rule from Constantinople in 688 when Justinian II and the caliph 'Abd al-Malik signed an unusual form of treaty neutralizing the island, which had been subject to Arab raids. For almost 300 years Cyprus was a kind of condominium of the Byzantine Empire and the Caliphate, and although the treaty was frequently violated by both sides, the arrangement lasted until 965, when the emperor Nicephorus II Phocas gained Cyprus completely for the Byzantines.

This appears to have been a period of modest prosperity. A remarkable mosaic of the 6th century, at Kiti, is the best example of Eastern Roman art of that date, comparable with works at Ravenna in Italy. Another equally remarkable mosaic of roughly the same date, at Lythrangomi, was destroyed in 1974. Wall paintings demonstrate close contact with Constantinople: those at Asinou, in particular, are noteworthy as being the earliest of an unparalleled series of mural paintings showing successive developments of Byzantine art.

In about 1185 a Byzantine governor of Cyprus, Isaac Comnenus, rebelled and proclaimed himself emperor. Isaac resisted attacks from the Byzantine emperors Andronicus I Comnenus and Isaac II Angelus, but in 1191, on engaging in hostilities with an English crusader fleet under King Richard I the Lion-Heart, he was defeated and imprisoned. The island was seized by Richard, from whom it was acquired by the crusading order of the Knights Templar; because they were unable to pay his price he took it back and sold it to Guy of Lusignan, the dispossessed king of Jerusalem.

Lusignan family

The noble family of Poitou (a province of western France) provided numerous crusaders and kings of Jerusalem, Cyprus, and Lesser Armenia. A branch of the family became counts of La Marche and Angoulême and played a role in precipitating the baronial revolt in England against King Henry III. The castle of Lusignan is associated with the medieval legend of Mélusine.

Hugh (Hugues) I, lord of Lusignan, was a vassal of the counts of Poitiers in the 10th century. Early members of the family participated in the Crusades, but it was Hugh VIII's sons who established the family fortunes.

Hugh VIII's eldest son and successor, Hugh IX the Brown (d. 1219), held the countship of La Marche. In 1200 his fiancée, Isabella of Angoulême, was taken for wife by his feudal lord, King John of England. This outrage caused Hugh to turn to the king of France, Philip II Augustus, forming an alliance that culminated in John's loss of his continental possessions.

John, in an attempt to pacify Hugh, gave his daughter Joan as fiancée to Hugh X (d. 1249), but the marriage never took place. Instead, after John's death, Hugh X married his widow, Isabella, in 1220. Hugh and Isabella fluctuated in their loyalty to John's successor (Isabella's son), Henry III.

When Louis IX of France granted Poitou as a countship to his brother Alphonse, Hugh at first supported him. Isabella's anger caused a turnabout and, eventually, brought about a disastrous revolt supported by Henry III. In this revolt Hugh lost his principal strongholds, but Louis IX pardoned the Lusignans, and they swore loyalty again.

Nine children were born to Isabella and Hugh X, five of whom went to England at the invitation of their half brother, Henry III. There they were rewarded with lands, riches, and distinctions at the expense of the English barons, who eventually revolted against Henry and forced the exile of the Lusignan brothers from England in 1258. Hugh XIII (d. 1303) pledged La Marche and Angoulême to Philip IV the Fair of France.

Two other sons of Hugh VIII became kings of Jerusalem and Cyprus. Guy (c. 1129-94), through his marriage to Sibyl, the sister of King Baldwin IV of Jerusalem, got the kingdom in 1186 but lost his capital city in wars with the Muslims (1187) and finally exchanged his empty title for the sovereignty of Cyprus (1192).

Guy's brother Amalric (Amaury) II (d. April 1, 1205) succeeded to the crown of Cyprus and became king of Jerusalem in 1197 by marrying Sibyl's sister Isabella after the death of her two previous husbands. Amalric was the founder of a dynasty of sovereigns of Cyprus lasting until 1475, when Cyprus was ceded to Venice. His descendants after 1269 regularly enjoyed the title of king of Jerusalem.

Among the most famous members of the house who ruled in Cyprus was Peter I (Pierre I; d. 1369), who set forth on various expeditions against the Muslims in a last attempt to gain the Holy Lands. He was assassinated by discontented nobles in Cyprus.

Hugh III

In French HUGUES, this is the king of Cyprus and Jerusalem who founded the house of Antioch-Lusignan that ruled Cyprus until 1489.

Succeeding his cousin Hugh II as king of Cyprus in 1267, he obtained the disputed crown of the dwindling crusader kingdom of Jerusalem two years later. The efforts of his rival, Charles I of Anjou, king of Sicily, who also claimed his rights to be a king of Jerusalem, and the resistance of his subjects prevented him from effectively establishing his authority in the Holy Land.

The Sixth Crusade

The failure of the Fifth Crusade placed a heavy responsibility on Frederick II. His motives as a crusader are difficult to assess. Always a controversial figure, he was to some the archenemy of the papacy, to others the greatest of emperors. His intellectual interests included Islam, and his attitude might seem to be more akin to that of the Eastern barons than the typical crusader from the West.

Through his marriage with John of Brienne's daughter Isabella (Yolande), he had a claim first to the kingship and then, on her death in 1228, to the regency of Jerusalem (Acre) for his son Conrad. As emperor he could claim a suzerainty over Cyprus by virtue of the cession by his predecessor Henry VI.

Frederick had finally agreed to terms that virtually placed his expedition under papal jurisdiction. Yet his entire Eastern policy was inextricably connected with his European concerns: Sicily, Italy and the papacy, and Germany. Cyprus-Jerusalem became, as a consequence, part of a greater imperial design.

Most of the fleet of the Sixth Crusade had left Italy in the late summer of 1227, but Frederick was delayed by illness. During the delay he received envoys from Sultan al-Kamil of Egypt, who, threatened by the ambitious designs of his Ayyubid brothers, was disposed to negotiate.

Meanwhile, Pope Gregory IX, less patient than his predecessor, had rejected the Emperor's plea of illness and excommunicated him. Thus, when Frederick departed in the summer of 1228 with the remainder of his forces, he was in the equivocal position of a crusader under the ban of the church. He arrived in Cyprus on July 21.

In Cyprus, John of Ibelin, the leading member of the influential Ibelin family, had been named regent for the young Henry I. Along with most of the other barons, he was willing to recognize the Emperor's rights as suzerain in Cyprus. But in Acre, since news of Isabel's death had arrived, the Emperor could claim only a regency for his infant son. John obeyed the Emperor's summons to meet him in Cyprus but despite intimidation refused to surrender his lordship of Beirut and insisted that his case be brought before the High

37

Court of barons. The matter was set aside, and Frederick left for Acre.

At Acre, Frederick met more opposition. News of his excommunication had arrived, and many refused to support him. Dependent, therefore, on the Teutonic Knights, an organization formed by Germans who remained in the east after an expedition in 1197 and now under the direction of Hermann of Salza, and his own small contingent of German crusaders, he was forced to attempt what he could by diplomacy. Negotiations, accordingly, were reopened with al-Kamil of Egypt.

The resulting treaty of 1229 is unique in the history of the Crusades. By diplomacy alone and without major military confrontation, Jerusalem, Bethlehem, and a corridor running to the sea were ceded to the Kingdom of Jerusalem. Exception was made for the Temple area, the Dome of the Rock, and the Aqsa Mosque, which the Muslims retained. The peace was to last for 10 years.

The benefits of the treaty of 1229 were more apparent than real. The areas ceded were not easily defensible, and Jerusalem soon became a prey to disorder. Furthermore, the treaty was denounced by the devout of both faiths. When Frederick, still under excommunication, entered the city, the Patriarch placed it under interdict. No priest was present, and Frederick placed a crown on his own head while one of the Teutonic Knights read the ceremony. Leaving agents in charge, he hastily returned to Europe and at San Germano made his peace with the Pope (July 23, 1230). Thereafter, his legal position was secure, and the Pope ordered the Patriarch to lift the interdict.

What followed in Jerusalem and Cyprus, however, was not orderly government by the Emperor's agents but civil war. For Frederick's imperial concept of government was totally opposed to the now well-established pre-eminence of the Jerusalem baronage. The barons of both Jerusalem and Cyprus, in alliance with the Genoese and a commune formed at Acre that elected John of Ibelin as mayor, resisted the imperial deputies, who had the support of the Pisans, the Teutonic Knights, Bohemond of Antioch, and a few nobles. The clergy, the other military orders, and the Venetians stood aloof.

The barons were able to win out in Cyprus, and in 1233 Henry I was recognized as king. Even after John of Ibelin, the "Old Lord of Beirut," died in 1236, the resistance continued. In 1243 a parliament at Acre refused homage to Frederick's son Conrad, unless he appeared in person, and named Alice, queen dowager of Cyprus, as regent.

Thus it was that baronial rule triumphed over imperial administration in the Levant. But the victory of the barons brought to the kingdom not strength but continued division, the more serious as new forces were appearing in the Muslim world. The Khwarezmian Turks, pushed south and west by the Mongols, had upset the power balance and gained the support of Egypt. After the 10 years' peace had expired in 1239, a poorly organized Crusade under Thibaut IV of Champagne and Richard of Cornwall accomplished little. In 1244 an alliance of Jerusalem and Damascus failed to prevent the capture and sack of Jerusalem by Khwarezmians with Egyptian aid. All the diplomatic gains of the preceding years were lost.

Lusignan kingdom, Genoese and Venetian rule

Guy, who called himself lord of Cyprus, invited families that had lost their lands in Palestine after the fall of Jerusalem to take up land in Cyprus. He thereby laid the basis for a feudal monarchy that survived to the end of the Middle Ages. His brother and successor, Amalric, obtained the title of king from the Holy Roman emperor Henry VI.

The earliest kings of the Lusignan dynasty were involved in the affairs of the small territory still left to the Kingdom of Jerusalem, and this commitment caused a heavy drain on the resources of Cyprus until the kingdom was extinguished in 1291 with the fall of Acre.

Over the next hundred years Cyprus enjoyed a reputation in Europe for immense riches where its nobles and merchants (especially Famagusta merchants) were concerned. Famagusta's opulence derived from its position as the last entrepôt for European trade adjacent to the Levant.

Crusading idea

The kings of Cyprus had kept alive the crusading idea, and the island remained a base for counterattack against the Muslims. In 1361 the Cypriot king Peter I (reigned 1359-69) devoted himself to the organization of a crusade. He captured Adalia (Antalya) on the Cilician coast of Anatolia, and in 1365, after collecting money and mercenaries in Western Europe, seized and sacked Alexandria. He was not able to maintain the conquest, however, and was soon forced to abandon Alexandria.

At his son's accession rivalry between Genoa and Venice, vying for control of Cyprus' valuable trade, resulted in Genoa's seizing Famagusta and holding it for almost a hundred years. This led to a rapid decline in the island's prosperity. In 1426 a marauding expedition from Egypt overran the island, which from then on paid tribute to Cairo. The last Lusignan king, James II (reigned 1460-73), a bastard of the royal house, seized the throne with the help of an Egyptian force and in 1464 expelled the Genoese from Famagusta.

He married a Venetian noblewoman, Caterina Cornaro. On his death, which was followed by that of his posthumous son, she succeeded him as the last queen of Cyprus (1474-89). During her reign she was under strong Venetian pressure and was eventually persuaded to cede Cyprus to the Venetian Republic. It remained a Venetian possession for 82 years until its capture by the Ottomans.

Buildings' survival

Many noteworthy buildings survive from the Lusignan and Venetian periods, in particular the Gothic cathedrals at Nicosia and Famagusta and the Abbey of Bellapais near Kyrenia. There are other Gothic churches throughout the island. Orthodox Christians also built numerous churches in a distinctive style, one often influenced by the Gothic, and the interiors illustrate the continued development of Byzantine art.

Cyprus also has imposing examples of medieval and Renaissance military architecture, such as the castles of Kyrenia, St. Hilarion, Buffavento, and Kantara and the elaborate Venetian fortifications of Nicosia and Famagusta.

Amalric II

Byname AMALRIC OF LUSIGNAN, French AMAURY, OR AMAURI, DE LUSIGNAN, this was the king of Cyprus (1194-1205) and of Jerusalem (1198-1205), who ably ruled the two separated kingdoms.

Amalric had been constable of Palestine before he was summoned by the Franks in Cyprus to become king there after the death of his brother Guy of Lusignan. Amalric planned a close alliance with Henry of Champagne, the uncrowned ruler of Palestine, betrothing his three sons to Henry's three daughters. He also became the vassal of the Holy Roman emperor Henry VI.

On Henry of Champagne's accidental death (1197), Amalric, a widower, was induced to marry Henry's widow, Queen Isabella I, because the emperor's German advisers were hoping to get the Latin kingdom of Jerusalem (then only a thin strip of the Palestinian coast) as a fief like Cyprus. Amalric, however, though he was crowned in 1198, decided to administer Jerusalem separately and to regard himself as merely its regent.

As king of Jerusalem, Amalric was able to make peace with his Muslim neighbours, thanks to the struggle that took place among them after Saladin's death in 1193. Though both sides periodically broke the treaty, it was renewed in September 1204 for six years. On Amalric's death Cyprus was left to his six-year-old son, Hugh, and the kingdom of Jerusalem remained in Isabella's possession.

Later Crusades and the Kingdom of Cyprus

Europe was dismayed by the disaster of 1291 but not surprised and shocked as it had been in 1187, for the end had been foreseen. Pope Nicholas IV had tried to organize aid before 1291, and he and his successors continued to do so afterward, but without success. France, which had always been the main bulwark of the Crusades, was in serious conflict with England, which eventually led to the Hundred Years' War in 1337.

Moreover, although it could scarcely have been understood at the time, Western Europe around 1300 was experiencing the first impact of a population decline and what proved to be a prolonged economic depression.

In the East, the military orders could no longer offer a standing nucleus of troops. In 1308 the Hospitallers took Rhodes and established their headquarters there. In 1344, with some assistance, they occupied Smyrna, which they held until 1402.

Meanwhile, the Teutonic Knights had moved their operations to the Baltic area. The Templars were less fortunate. In 1308 the French Templars were arrested by Philip IV, and in 1312 the order was suppressed by Pope Clement V.

It is not surprising, therefore, that such response as did follow papal urgings was largely in the form of Crusade theories. For some years after 1291 various projects were elaborated, all designed to avoid previous mistakes and explore new tactics.

The Franciscan missionary Ramon Llull (died 1315), for example, in his *Liber de fine*, suggested a campaign of informed preaching as well as military force. Pierre Dubois (*c.* 1305-07) submitted a detailed scheme for a Crusade to be directed by Philip IV of France, and in 1321 Marino Sanudo in his *Secreta fidelium crucis* produced an elaborate plan for an economic blockade of Egypt. But none of these or any other such schemes was put into effect.

King Peter I of Cyprus finally organized an expedition that in 1365 succeeded in a temporary occupation of Alexandria. After a horrible sack and massacre, the unruly crusaders returned to Cyprus with immense booty.

Peter planned to return, but no European aid was forthcoming, and after his murder in 1369 a treaty of peace was signed. No further crusades set out with Jerusalem as the objective. What followed were not really crusades in the old sense but campaigns such as the crusades of Nicopolis in 1396 and Varna in 1444, whose purpose was to defend Europe against the Ottoman Turks, a new power in the East.

With the failure of all attempts to regain a foothold on the mainland, Cyprus remained the sole crusader outpost, and after 1291 the island kingdom was faced with a serious refugee problem.

It was in Cyprus that many of the institutions established by the Franks survived. For, although Jerusalem and Cyprus normally had separate governments, through intermarriage and the exigencies of diplomacy the histories of the two had become interwoven.

Regents of one were often chosen from among relatives in the other. It has been noted that many Jerusalem barons resided in Cyprus.

With suitable modifications, the *Assises de Jérusalem* applied on the island. As on the mainland, the French character of the Cypriot Latins is evident in the remains of Gothic structures.

In one respect Cyprus did differ from the mainland. Whereas the First Kingdom had established a reasonable modus vivendi with its native population, such was not the case in the island kingdom. Many Greek landholders had fled, and those who remained apparently suffered a loss of status.

All Greeks resisted the Latinizing efforts of the early 13th-century popes and their representatives. Innocent IV was more flexible, but tension persisted until the Turkish conquest in the 16th century.

Cornaro, Caterina

(Born in 1454 in Venice, died in 1510)

This Venetian noblewoman became queen of Cyprus by marrying James II, king of Cyprus, Jerusalem, and Armenia, supplying him with a much-needed alliance with Venice.

The marriage agreement was reached in 1468, but in the next four years James considered other possible alliances by way of marriage, especially with Naples. In 1472, Caterina finally departed for Cyprus, where the formal ceremony took place.

James died in 1473, leaving her and her unborn child heirs to the kingdom. Unsuccessful plotters against James now conspired to deprive Caterina of the throne; and when she bore a son, James III (August 1473), Cyprus was seized by the archbishop of Nicosia and his Neapolitan allies. Imprisoned briefly, Caterina was restored by the intervention of Venice.

The early death of Caterina's son (1474) precipitated further conspiracies, all of which were foiled by the Venetians, who gradually usurped Caterina's power and finally forced the queen to abdicate (1489). She was received with honour at Venice and given the castle and town of Asolo, which she governed beneficently. She died after having fled Asolo when her castle was occupied by imperial troops.

6. EARLY CHRISTIANITY

Christian belief

Undoubtedly the most important event in the Roman period was the introduction of Christianity. The Apostle Paul accompanied by Barnabas (later St. Barnabas), a native of the Cypriot Jewish community, preached there in about AD 45 and converted the proconsul, Sergius Paulus. By the time of Constantine I the Great, Christians were numerous in the island and may have constituted a majority.

Church of Cyprus

Also called ORTHODOX CHURCH OF CYPRUS, is one of the oldest autocephalous, or ecclesiastically independent, churches of the Eastern Orthodox communion. Its independence first recognized by the third ecumenical Council of Ephesus (431), was reaffirmed by the Council in Trullo (692) and was never lost, not even during the occupation of the island by the crusaders.

Under the feudal French dynasty of the Lusignans (1191-1489) and the Venetians (1489-1571), the efforts of the Latin bishops to submit the Orthodox Church of Cyprus to the pope's authority were unsuccessful. Until the Turkish conquest of the island in 1571, the Greek bishops were often submitted to the authority of the Latin archbishop and forced to serve as auxiliaries of their Latin colleagues.

The highest ecclesiastical authority lay with the synod, composed of the archbishop of Nicosia and the three other bishops of the island--Paphos, Citium, and Kyrenia--who were, and still are, elected by both clergy and laity, each of the four bishoprics being divided into several parishes.

The bishops became the natural leaders of national resistance: during the Greek War of Independence (1821-32), all the bishops on the island, as well as several abbots, were hanged by the Turks, while in the years of British control (1878-1958), the bishops took an active lead in the Greek Cypriot movement for union with Greece (*énosis*).

44

In 1956 the Archbishop Makarios and the Bishop of Kyrenia were exiled by the British. When the new Cypriot republic became independent in 1960, the church was assured of its position as an autocephalous and independent Greek Orthodox Church on the basis of its old titles, and Archbishop Makarios was elected the first president of the new republic.

Monastic life has developed greatly since the beginning of the republic. There are several monasteries, the most important being the monastery of Kykkou. Parish clergy are educated in an undergraduate seminary; higher theological education is obtained at the University of Athens. The church keeps several educational and philanthropic institutions and publishes *Apostolos Barnabas,* a monthly ecclesiastical-theological review.

Saint Hilarion

(Born circa AD 291, in Tabatha, Palestine, near modern Gaza, died in 371, in Cyprus.)

A monk and mystic who founded Christian monasticism in Palestine modelled after the Egyptian tradition.

Most knowledge about Hilarion derives from a semi-legendary and rhetorically embellished account of his life written about 391 by the Latin biblical scholar St. Jerome, using material by Bishop Epiphanius of Constantia (now Salamis, Cyprus), and an influential 4th-century theologian-chronicler. Jerome greatly exaggerated Hilarion's importance in order to glorify Palestinian monasticism, to which he himself belonged. Despite a historical nucleus, therefore, it is often difficult to determine the facts.

According to Jerome, Hilarion came from non-Christian parents and studied under a grammarian at Alexandria, where he became a Christian. He also came under the influence of the renowned desert ascetic Anthony of Egypt and followed his discipline for two months. Returning to Palestine in 306 at the age of 15, he instituted the eremitical life there by erecting a hut in the wilderness some seven miles from Maiuma, near Gaza, on the road to Egypt. He observed the strict ascetical regimen of fasting and chanting the Old Testament psalm prayers, and, like the Egyptian hermits, he wove baskets of rushes to earn his subsistence, possessing only a monk's garb, which he willed to a colleague at death.

45

Jerome's account emphasizes Hilarion's proselytizing the Saracens and his wonder-working among the sick and demoniacs. After establishing the first Palestinian monastery in 329, Hilarion, seeking solitude, migrated to the monastic centre at Thebes, Egypt, thence through North Africa and Sicily, eventually settling in Cyprus. He is credited with prophesying the religious persecution decreed by Emperor Julian the Apostate (361-363). After death, his body was recovered by the monks of his original foundation in Gaza. A cult of veneration spread to Europe, especially about Venice and Pisa, Italy, and in parts of France.

Orthodox Church in Middle East

As a result of the Greco-Turkish War, the entire Greek population of Asia Minor was transferred to Greece (1922); the Orthodox under the immediate jurisdiction of the ecumenical patriarchate of Constantinople were thus reduced to the Greek population of Istanbul and its vicinity.

This population, rapidly shrinking in recent years, is now reduced to a few thousand. Still recognized as holding an honorary primacy among the Orthodox churches, the ecumenical patriarchate also exercises jurisdiction over several dioceses of the "diaspora" and, by consent of the Greek government, over the Greek islands.

The impressive personality of Patriarch Athenagoras I (1948-72), who was succeeded by Dimitrios, contributed to its prestige on the pan-Orthodox and ecumenical levels. The patriarchate convened pan-Orthodox conferences in Rhodes, Belgrade, Geneva, and other cities and began preparations for a "Great Council" of the Orthodox Church.

Together with the ecumenical patriarchate, the ancient sees of Alexandria, Antioch, and Jerusalem are remnants of the Byzantine imperial past, but under the present conditions they still possess many opportunities of development: Alexandria, as the centre of emerging African communities (see below The Orthodox diaspora and missions); Antioch, as the largest Arab Christian group, with dioceses in Syria, Lebanon, and Iraq; and Jerusalem, as the main custodian of the Christian holy places in that city.

The two ancient churches of Cyprus and Georgia, with their quite peculiar history, continue to play important roles among the

Orthodox sister churches. Autocephalous since 431, the Church of Cyprus survived the successive occupations, and often oppressions, by the Arabs, the Crusaders, the Venetians, the Turks, and the English.

Following the pattern of all areas where Islam was predominant, the archbishop is traditionally seen as the ethnarch of the Greek Christian Cypriots. Archbishop Makarios also became the first president of the independent Republic of Cyprus in 1960.

The Church of Georgia, isolated in the Caucasus in a country that became part of the Russian Empire in 1801, is the witness of one of the most ancient Christian traditions. It received autocephaly from its mother Church of Antioch as early as the 6th century and developed a literary and artistic civilization in its own language. Its head bears the traditional title of "Catholicos-Patriarch."

When the Russians annexed the country in 1801, they suppressed Georgia's autocephaly and the church was governed by a Russian "exarch" until 1917 when the Georgians re-established their ecclesiastical independence. Fiercely persecuted during the 1920s, the Georgian Church survives to the present day as an autocephalous patriarchate.

7. CYPRIOT KINGDOMS

Ptolemy IX Soter II

Byname LATHYRUS (GREEK: CHICKPEA), Macedonian king of Egypt (reigned 116-110, 109-107, and 88-81 BC) who, after ruling Cyprus and Egypt in various combinations with his brother, Ptolemy X Alexander I, and his mother, Cleopatra III, widow of Ptolemy VIII Euergetes II, gained sole rule of the country in 88 and sought to keep Egypt from excessive Roman influence while trying to develop trade with the East.

The unusual will of Euergetes II partitioned Egypt's possessions, leaving Cleopatra III as the effective ruler of Egypt and Cyprus. Although she preferred his younger brother, Ptolemy Alexander, popular sentiment forced the dowager queen to dismiss him and to associate Ptolemy Soter on the throne with herself.

After compelling the king in 115 to divorce his strong-willed sister-queen, Cleopatra IV, his mother forced Ptolemy to marry his younger, more pliable sister, Cleopatra Selene. The next year, after his brother was sent to Cyprus as governor, Ptolemy Soter appeared with his mother as joint ruler of Egypt.

The latent hostility between the son and his mother finally erupted in October 110, when Cleopatra expelled him from Egypt and recalled his brother from Cyprus. Soter II returned in early 109 but was evicted anew by his mother in March of the following year.

After a reconciliation in May 108 he fled a third time and established himself in Cyprus, from where in 107 he invaded northern Syria to assist one of the claimants to the Seleucid empire, while his mother, allying herself with the Jewish king in Palestine, actively aided another Seleucid pretender. During the protracted war his mother died (101) and Ptolemy X Alexander became the sole ruler of Egypt, while Soter II remained entrenched in Cyprus.

After Alexander's unpopularity drove him from Alexandria a second time and he perished at sea, Soter returned to resume sole rule over Egypt. Lacking a queen, he brought back his brother's widow, who was also his own daughter, Berenice III, and associated her on the throne with himself. Shortly before Soter's return in 88 a serious native rebellion erupted around Thebes in Upper Egypt. After three years of hard fighting Thebes capitulated and was sacked in retribution.

Ptolemy Soter refused to give aid to the Romans in the course of their war with Pontus, a Black Sea kingdom, and after the Roman sack of Athens in 88 the Egyptian rulers helped rebuild the city, for which commemorative statues of them were erected. Ptolemy IX died in 81, leaving his daughter and widow as his successor.

Hellenistic and Roman rule

Alexander allowed the Cypriot kingdoms to continue but took from them the right of coinage. After his death in 323 BC Cyprus was contested by his successors; the eventual victor was Ptolemy I of Egypt, who suppressed the kingdoms and made the island a province of his Egyptian kingdom. He forced the last king of Salamis, Nicocreon, to commit suicide in 310 BC, together with all his family; their cenotaph, a particularly fine specimen containing ornaments and clay effigies of the royal families, has been discovered. For two and a half centuries Cyprus remained a Ptolemaic possession, ruled by a strategus, or governor-general.

Cyprus as a Roman province

Cyprus was annexed by the Roman Republic in 58 BC and, along with Cilicia on the coast of Anatolia, was made into a Roman province. The orator and writer Cicero was one of its first proconsuls.

Cyprus was briefly retroceded to Cleopatra VII of Egypt by Julius Caesar, and this status was confirmed by Mark Antony, but after the victory of Caesar's heir, Octavian (subsequently the emperor Augustus), over Mark Antony and Cleopatra at Actium in 31 BC it became a Roman possession again.

It was originally administered as part of the "imperial" province of Syria but became a separate "senatorial" province in 22 BC in consequence of the constitutional settlement of the previous year. Its governors resumed the old republican title of proconsul, although there is evidence that Augustus could, and on one occasion did, influence the Senate's choice.

For the next 600 years Cyprus enjoyed a profound peace, disturbed only by occasional earthquakes and epidemics and by a Jewish uprising put down by a lieutenant of the future emperor Hadrian in AD 116. Many large public buildings were erected: among them were a gymnasium and theatre at Salamis, a theatre at Curium, and the governor's palace at Paphos.

Salamis

Salamis was a principal city of ancient Cyprus, located on the east coast of the island, north of modern Famagusta. According to the Homeric epics, Salamis was founded after the Trojan War by the archer Teucer, who came from the island of Salamis, off Attica. This literary tradition probably reflects the Sea Peoples' occupation of Cyprus (*c.* 1193 BC), Teucer perhaps representing Tjekker of the Egyptian records. Later, the city grew because of its excellent harbour; it became the chief Cypriot outlet for trade with Phoenicia, Egypt, and Cilicia.

Salamis came under Persian control in 525 BC. In 306 BC Demetrius I Poliorcetes of Macedonia won a great naval victory there over Ptolemy I of Egypt. Salamis was sacked in the Jewish revolt of AD 115-117 and suffered repeatedly from earthquakes; it was completely rebuilt by the Christian emperor Constantius II (reigned AD 337-361) and given the name Constantia. Under Christian rule, Salamis was the metropolitan see of Cyprus. Destroyed again by the Arabs under Mu'awiyah (*c.* 648), the city was thereafter abandoned.

Evagoras

(Died in 374 BC)

Evagoras was the king of Salamis, in Cyprus, *c.* 410-374 BC, whose policy was one of friendship with Athens and the promotion of Hellenism in Cyprus; he eventually fell under Persian domination.

Most of what is known of him is found in the panegyric "Evagoras" by Isocrates, where he is described, with extravagant praise, as a model ruler whose aim was to promote the welfare of his state by cultivation of Greek refinement and civilization. Evagoras' services to Athens were recognized by the gift of Athenian citizenship.

For a time he also maintained friendly relations with Achaemenian Persia, securing Persian support for Athens in the early years of the

Corinthian War (395-387) against Sparta. He participated, along with the Persian fleet, in the naval victory over Sparta off Cnidus (394), but from 391 Evagoras and the Persians were virtually at war.

Aided by the Athenians and the Egyptians, Evagoras extended his rule over the greater part of Cyprus and to several cities of Anatolia. When Athens withdrew its support after the peace of Antalcides (386), Evagoras' troops fought without allies until they were crushed at Citium (Larnaca, Cyprus) in 381.

He fled to Salamis, where he managed to conclude a peace that allowed him to remain nominally king of Salamis, though in reality he was a vassal of the Achaemenian king. He was assassinated by a eunuch.

Greek immigration

The mass immigration of Greek-speaking peoples from the Peloponnese began with the Iron Age (1100-700 BC). From the start of the 1st millennium the Greek language has been dominant in Cyprus; the fact that the dialectal form in which it first appears is known as Arcado-Cypriot confirms traditions of the Peloponnesian origin--and specifically of the Arcadian origin--of the immigrants.

They founded new cities, which became the capitals of six ancient Greek kingdoms on Cyprus: Curium (Greek Kourion), Paphos, Marion, Soli (Greek Soloi), Lapithos, and Salamis. In about 800 BC a Phoenician colony was founded at Citium (Greek Kition), near modern Larnaca. The colony was a dependency of the mother city, Tyre.

A seventh kingdom, that of Amathus, remained for some time under the control of the earlier indigenous inhabitants; the language used there was called Eteo-Cypriot ("True Cypriot") by the Greeks. Amathus was active politically, especially in external trade relations.

The later Iron Age was a period of advancing civilization, as evidenced by the spectacular chariot-burials of the royal family of Salamis, which so closely match descriptions in the Homeric poems as to suggest inspiration by them.

8. CYPRIOT SYLLABARY AND GREEK INFLUENCE

This was a system of writing used on the island of Cyprus, chiefly from the 6th to the 3rd century BC. The syllabary consists of 56 signs, each of which represents a different syllable. Most inscriptions written with this syllabary are in the Greek language, although the syllabary was originally designed for writing the earlier non-Greek language of Cyprus.

The classical Cypriot syllabary is apparently a late development of the still undeciphered Cypro-Minoan script (containing 63 syllabic symbols), which was found on a number of clay tablets from Cyprus and Syria and dates from about 1500 to about 1100 BC. The Cypro-Minoan script in turn is thought to be a distant offshoot of the early Cretan scripts (Linear A and Linear B).

Dialects

Among the dialects there are a West group, an Aeolic group, an Arcado-Cypriot group, and an Ionic-Attic group. Modern scholars have tried in various ways to combine some of these groups--for example, by considering Aeolic and Arcado-Cypriot as varieties of "central" Greek or by considering Arcado-Cypriot and Ionic-Attic as varieties of "southern" Greek and West Greek and Aeolic as varieties of "northern" Greek.

Early Helladic and Early Cypriot

Mainland Greece probably received its Bronze Age settlers from the Cyclades, but the two cultures soon diverged. A prosperous era arose about 2500 BC and lasted until about 2200. Sculpture was overshadowed by pottery, metalwork, and architecture among the Early Helladic arts.

In the Early Cypriot, the only surviving sculptures are a series of steatite cruciform figures of a mother goddess (3000-2500 BC) stylized in much the same way as contemporary Cycladic idols, from which they may have been derived.

Middle Cycladic, Middle Helladic, and Middle Cypriot

During the Middle Cycladic period, the Cyclades suffered a diminution in prosperity and seem to have become politically

52

subordinate to Crete. Two waves of Indo-European peoples seem to have descended on the Greek mainland, one about 2200 BC and the other about 2000 BC. They destroyed much and for long contributed little to Greece's artistic heritage.

The pottery of this period, however, is of high quality. The Middle Cypriot period was a development of the Early Cypriot. As on the mainland, no important art apart from pottery has survived.

Late Cypriot period

Cyprus reached its highest degree of prosperity in the Late Cypriot period, due to increased exploitation of its copper mines. There were close commercial relations not only with the Levant coast, as before, but also with Egypt, Crete, and Mycenaean Greece (the latter being close from 1400 BC).

About 1200 BC Mycenaean Greeks, refugees from their homeland, settled in Cyprus. They introduced their skills and produced many luxury articles in a mixed Mycenaean-Cypriot style. Cyprus escaped the invasions that finally destroyed Mycenaean and Minoan culture, but its own culture did not last much longer. By 1050 BC, for reasons that are not clear, it, too, had ceased to exist.

As in Crete, large-scale sculpture was rejected in favour of small-scale work. A bronze figure of a horned god (shortly after 1200 BC) from Enkomi (Cyprus Museum, Nicosia) shows a successful blend of Mycenaean and Cypriot elements. A good example of these characteristics is a carved ivory gaming box (British Museum), also from Enkomi, whose style shows a blend of Mycenaean and Middle Eastern motifs.

Zeno of Citium

(Born circa 335 BC, in Citium, died circa 263, in Athens.)

This is the Greek thinker who founded the Stoic school of philosophy, which influenced the development of philosophical and ethical thought in Hellenistic and Roman times.

He went to Athens c. 312 BC and attended lectures by the Cynic philosophers Crates of Thebes and Stilpon of Megara, in addition to lectures at the Academy.

Arriving at his own philosophy, he began to teach in the Stoa Poikile (Painted Colonnade), whence the name of his philosophy. Zeno's philosophical system included logic and theory of knowledge, physics, and ethics--the latter being central.

He taught that happiness lay in conforming the will to the divine reason, which governs the universe. In logic and the theory of knowledge he was influenced by Antisthenes and Diodorus Cronus, in physics by Heracleitus. None of his many treatises, written in harsh but forceful Greek, has survived save in fragmentary quotations.

Trade

Foreign manufactures reaching the Aegean and especially Crete during the Bronze Age included Cypriot pottery, Mesopotamian and other Oriental cylinder seals, and Egyptian stone vases, ivories, and scarabs, while Cretan and eventually Mycenaean pottery is found in Egypt and elsewhere in the Levant.

By the 14th and 13th centuries, Mycenaean pottery is found densely in the Levant; it is often accompanied by Cypriot pottery as though carried in Cypriot or Syrian ships. Mycenaean pottery not mixed with Cypriot pottery is found in Anatolia from Troy to Tarsus.

Because there is almost nothing on the mainland in return, one may suppose that trade was carried on in archaeological invisibles, such as food, textiles, copper ores, and perhaps slaves or war captives (some are attested in the Linear B texts). Mycenaeans may also have exported technology, such as weapon making, or mercenaries. Crete and the mainland had to import tin for bronze, probably from Anatolia, and both used copper ores from Cyprus and other sources.

Minoan contact seems to have reached Sicily and Sardinia, and metal ingots may have been brought back from the west. Silver-lead was produced in the Cyclades and Attica. The Kas Ulu Burun shipwreck shows an extensive trade in glass ingots, often cobalt blue, as well. Ostrich eggs and stone for making vases were among imports to Crete from Egypt, and ivory came from there or from Syria.

Amber from the Baltic reached the mainland in some quantity during the Shaft Grave Period and later but is rarely found in Crete. Exports from the Aegean may have included woollen goods, olive oil, and timber, as well as silver. In Crete, at any rate, foreign trade may have been largely under palace control, but a class of private merchants engaged in overseas commerce no doubt existed in the Aegean.

Soli

In Greek SOLOI, this ancient Greek city on Cyprus was located west of modern Karavostasi on Morphou Bay. Soli traditionally was founded after the Trojan War by the Attic hero Acamas, perhaps reflecting the Sea Peoples' occupation of Cyprus (c. 1193 BC).

According to another legend, however, the city was named for the Athenian lawgiver Solon (flourished 6th century BC), who was supposed to have visited Cyprus. Soli was probably an ally of Assyria in the 7th century BC.

In Hellenic times the city had little political importance, though its copper mines were famous. Excavated monuments include a theatre, a temple of Aphrodite and Isis, and a 5th-century palace situated 5 miles (8 km) west of the town at Vouni.

Amathus

This was the ancient city located near Limassol, Cyprus. among sandy hills and sand dunes, which may explain its name (Greek amathos, "sand"). Founded by the Phoenicians (c. 1500 BC), Amathus maintained strong sympathies with the Phoenician mainland and refused to join various Cypriot revolts against Persia.

When the rest of Cyprus was annexed to Egypt after the death of Alexander the Great, Amathus resisted annexation. It derived its wealth from grain and from copper mines. Its temple of Adonis and Aphrodite was famous in Roman times, hence the Latin epithet Amathusia applied to Venus. The city still flourished in the 7th century AD but was almost deserted by the 12th century.

Idalium

Also called IDALION, this ancient city in southern Cyprus was situated near modern Dali. Of pre-Greek origin, Idalium was one of

10 Cypriot kingdoms listed on the prism (many-sided tablet) of the Assyrian king Esarhaddon (680-669 BC).

Eventually dominated by the Phoenician city of Citium, it became the centre of a cult of Aphrodite and of the Greco-Phoenician deity Resheph-Apollo. A terra-cotta model found there (now in the Louvre) is believed to represent the Resheph-Apollo temple.

Pygmalion

In Greek mythology, a king of Cyprus who fell in love with a statue of the goddess Aphrodite. The Roman poet Ovid, in his *Metamorphoses,* invented a more sophisticated version: Pygmalion, a sculptor, made an ivory statue representing his ideal of womanhood and then fell in love with his own creation; the goddess Venus brought the statue to life in answer to his prayer.

Solon, Later years

Among the places Solon visited were Egypt and Cyprus. These visits are attested by his poems. Less credible (because of chronological difficulties) is the famous encounter with the fabulously rich Croesus, king of Lydia, who, so the story goes, learned from Solon that wealth and power were not happiness and that, so long as he was alive, no man could be counted happy.

When Solon returned, he found the citizens divided into regional factions headed by prominent nobles. Of these, his friend Peisistratus, general in the final war for Salamis and leader of northeastern Attica, seemed to Solon to be planning to become tyrant.

The old statesman's urgent warnings were disregarded, even dismissed as the ravings of a madman. His reply was that "A little time will show the citizens my madness, when truth comes in our midst." It was not long before he was proved right: Peisistratus did become tyrant (560 BC). Although on this occasion he was soon ejected, it seems that Solon did not live to see it.

9. PERSIAN, ASSYRIAN AND EGYPTIAN EMPIRES

In 525 BC the Cypriot kings transferred their allegiance to the Achaemenid (Persian) conquerors of Egypt. The Cypriots retained their independence until the accession of Darius I (522 BC) but were then incorporated into the fifth satrapy of the Persian Empire.

When the Ionians revolted in 499 BC all the kingdoms of Cyprus except Amathus joined them; the revolt was suppressed in about a year's campaigning, culminating in sieges of Paphos and Soli. In Xerxes I's invasion of Greece in 480 BC the Cypriot kings, like the Ionians, contributed naval contingents to his forces.

During the 5th century Cyprus remained under Persian rule in spite of a major Athenian expedition there in 450/449 BC. Evagoras, who became king of Salamis in 411 BC, maintained a pro-Hellenic policy, with some help from Athens, and succeeded in extending his rule over a large part of the island. He was defeated by the Persians in 381 BC and was assassinated in 374 BC.

After the victory of Alexander the Great over the last Achaemenid ruler, Darius III, at Issus in 333 BC, the Cypriot kings rallied to Alexander and assisted him at the siege of Tyre. During the period from 475 to 325 BC, known conventionally as the Classical Period, Cypriot art came under strong Attic influence.

Assyrian and Egyptian domination

In 709 BC Sargon II of Assyria erected a stela at Citium recording the fact that seven Cypriot kings had paid him homage; subsequent Assyrian documents speak of 11 tributary kingdoms, the seven already mentioned plus Citium, Kyrenia, Tamassos, and Idalium.

This subordination to Assyria, probably rather nominal, lasted until about 663 BC. For the next hundred years Cyprus enjoyed a period of complete independence and exuberant development.

Epic poetry was greatly popular, as it had always been, and much was written on the island; Stasinus of Cyprus, credited with the authorship of the lost epic poem *Cypria*, was reckoned among the most important poets in this style in the 7th century.

Bronze work and ironwork, a spirited style of ceramic decoration, and delicate jewellery and ivory work are characteristic of this period; among outstanding works are the sumptuous ivory throne and bedstead excavated from a royal tomb at Salamis dated from about 700 BC.

When the Assyrian Empire finally broke up at the end of the 7th century BC, Egypt, under the Saite dynasty, became the predominant power in the eastern Mediterranean.

In about 569 BC the Cypriot kingdoms recognized the pharaoh Ahmose II as their overlord. Direct Egyptian influence was not always apparent, although many limestone sculptures reproduce Egyptian conventions in dress and some statues are directly inspired by Egyptian models.

A more important influence in the last years of the Archaic period (750-475 BC) came from the artistic schools of Ionia. From the same source probably came the inspiration for the issue of coinage; the first Cypriot coins were struck for Euelthon, king of Salamis (560-525 BC).

Citium

In Greek KITION, principal Phoenician city in Cyprus situated on the southeast coast near modern Larnaca.

The earliest remains at Citium are those of an Aegean colony of the Mycenaean Age (*c.* 1400-1100 BC). The biblical name Kittim, representing Citium, was also used for Cyprus as a whole.

A Phoenician dedication to the god "Baal of Lebanon," found at Citium, suggests that the city may have belonged to Tyre; and an official monument of the Assyrian king Sargon II indicates that Citium was the administrative centre of Cyprus during the Assyrian protectorate (709-*c.* 668 BC).

During the Greek revolts of 499, 386 and following years, and 353 BC, Citium led the side loyal to Persia. It remained an important city even after Alexander the Great conquered Persia. Citium suffered repeatedly from earthquakes, however, and in medieval times its harbour became silted and the population moved to Larnaca.

Bronze ages

After the Chalcolithic Age, dating from 3000 to 2500 BC, began the Bronze Ages, which in Cypriot archaeology are treated as separate from the Chalcolithic and which lasted for about 1,500 years.

The Middle Bronze Age (1900-1600 BC) produced several styles of well-made and competently decorated pottery, and its bronze implements show a well-advanced craftsmanship; imports from Crete, Anatolia, Syria, and Egypt prove that external trade had begun. It has been conjectured that the name Alashiya or Alasia, which occurs in Hittite and Egyptian records in connection with the supply of copper, refers to Cyprus.

These trade links probably account for the foundation of the new settlements in the east of the island that were to develop into international urban emporiums.

The Late Bronze Age (1600-1050 BC) was one of the most formative periods of the life of ancient Cyprus. The island s international contacts extended from the Aegean Sea to the Levant and the Nile Delta. (Thutmose III of Egypt claimed Cyprus as one of his conquests in about 1500 BC.)

Writing, in the form of a linear script known as Cypro-Minoan, was borrowed from Crete. Cypriot craftsmen were distinguished for fine jewellery, ivory carving, and bronze figures. From about 1400 BC a profusion of Mycenaean pottery was imported from mainland Greece, and it is possible that Mycenaean artists accompanied the merchants. After 1200 BC, with the collapse of Mycenaean civilization, there is evidence of Greek immigration from the Peloponnese.

The principal city, and port, was Engomi (west of Famagusta); its massive city walls and houses of hewn stone are evidence of a high degree of prosperity.

10. MODERN HISTORY

EOKA (Greek Organisation of Cypriot Fighters)

Until 1974 the population of Cyprus was approximately 80% Greek Cypriot, 18% Turkish Cypriot, with the other 2% made up of other nationalities. The two main groups lived in all parts of the island. There were Greek & Turkish villages throughout the island - it was not the case that the Greeks lived in the south and the Turks in the north, and indeed Kyrenia was an overwhelmingly Greek Cypriot town.

From 1878 until independence in 1960, Cyprus was a British colony. In 1954 a campaign started by the right wing of Greek Cypriots for union with Greece, "Enosis". The organisation for this 'revolution' was led by EOKA (Greek Organisation of Cypriot Fighters – Ellinikos Organismos Kyprion Agoniston), which fought the British army. This secret organisation of EOKA was financed by the autonomous Orthodox church of Cyprus and secrecy led by Archbishop Makarios.

A few years later the British Governor became suspicious and Makarios was exiled to Seychelles.

As Turkey was favouring the partition (taksim) of the island, they openly opposed the Greeks in their idea of gaining union (Enosis) with Greece. To this effect, the British government took advantage of the situation and recruited Turkish Cypriots into the police force to help in their campaign against EOKA. This increased the tension and hostility between the two communities.

Following the six years of the EOKA campaign, Britain, Turkey and the coerced Greeks of mainland Greece imposed independence on the Cypriots with a constitution which gave the Turkish Cypriots power and influence way beyond their proportion of the population, and a veto on most decisions. The 'independence' constitution did not work, which led to problems between the communities through the 1960s right up to 1974.

Turkish invasion

In 1974 Greece was led by a military junta - the Colonels. They initiated a coup in July 1974, replacing president Makarios with an ultra right winger-nationalist EOKA leader who still sought Enosis.

This led directly to a Turkish invasion on 21 July 1974. Although there were numerous UN resolutions for Turkey to stop the invasion and their armed forces to withdraw, Turkey ignored all the international requests. By this time, the Turkish forces occupied 38% of the island, and made a quarter of a million Greek Cypriots refugees, who fled south as the Turkish army advanced.

The northern 38% of Cyprus is still under Turkish army occupation, with the island divided by a so-called green line. Until recently there was only one official crossing point - the Ledra Palace hotel in Nicosia.

As such, Cyprus remains divided, the only European country, following the re-unification of Berlin.

The Turkish-occupied north is like a time-warp; the modernisation of Cyprus has left the Turkish occupied north behind, and numerous former Greek Cypriot villages are now merely Turkish army camps, and Turkish army convoys are the most frequent vehicles on the roads.

Despite the 39 years of occupation the forces of occupation make their presence felt even at the most famous historical sites. Both the flag of the Muslim Turkish occupying forces, and their northern puppet-state, fly above this Greek Christian Orthodox abbeys and churches.

Many of the resort hotels remain as they were left by the bombing of the Turkish air force in August 1974, while the rest of the holiday resorts which were undamaged by the fighting have been fenced off, kept out-of-bounds and left to rot for the last 39 years. The surprising thing is that some people even go to this place for their holidays - it is doubtful if these properties and historical sites will ever be returned to their original Greek owners.

In November 2002 the UN began another determined attempt to re-unite Cyprus, through the UN *'Annan plan'*. This was discussed through the winter, and a revised version was thrashed out by the

President of Cyprus and Rauf Denktash leader of the Turkish occupied north of Cyprus.

After face to face negotiations and despite several demonstrations of up to 100,000 Turkish Cypriots in favour of a settlement in the north, Denktash finally rejected the settlement proposals and declared the occupied part of Cyprus as an independent country, recognised only by Turkey.

Despite the continuing division, on May 1, 2004, the European Union accepted Cyprus as a member of the EU. In view of this, the Government of Cyprus lifted the trade embargo with the north that had existed since 1974. They began actively encouraging Turkish Cypriots (unemployment in the north is over 50%) to apply to work in the south, and for southern businesses to trade with the north.

Cyprus enters the EU

The approach of Cyprus' entry to the EU on 1 May 2004 renewed the effort to re-unite Cyprus. The *'Annan plan'* was taken off the shelf, dusted down and renewed efforts were made to reach a settlement based upon it. Some changes to the original plan were agreed, but it still proved impossible to get the Greek & Turkish Cypriots to agree. In the end, with the support of both Greece & Turkey, the United Nations arranged for a referendum to be held in both parts of Cyprus on 24 April.

The campaign in the Republic was fierce, with the President making an emotional appeal on TV for a no vote, the Greek Cypriots took most of the rest of the world by surprise and voted no, whereas the Turkish Cypriots voted yes. This result was treaded with dismay by both the EU and the UN. It seemed to many that after being regarded as the injured party for 30 years by voting no the Greek Cypriots had succeeded overnight in making the Turkish Cypriots the injured party, with all the international sympathy transferred to them.

The outcome was a puzzle to many who could not understand why after 30 years of seeking a settlement, the Greek Cypriots should turn their back upon it when the opportunity arose. There is a very simple answer. The majority of Greek Cypriots said no simply because they were not prepared to legitimise the presence of Turkish troops on Cyprus, that same Turkish army which in the summer of 1974 had invaded their island and made so many of them refugees.

Cyprus joins the Euro

The years from January 2004 to April 2013 have seen very mixed fortunes for the modern history of Cyprus. The first 4 years saw optimism about the future increase rapidly, and with it the accelerating pace of uncontrolled and excessive development – everyone wanted to cash in on the boom. Too many houses were built, often without any regard for the infrastructure around new developments. Some were done well, others were a mess.

At the beginning of 2008 Cyprus made the mistake of joining the Euro. Just as the world financial crisis was beginning it was the worst possible time to join a fixed exchange mechanism over which the country had neither control nor influence. The conversion rate for Cyprus pounds in Euros was far too high, and led to severe inflation. Items that were priced at 10 Cyprus pounds were converted to a price of 17 Euros, which soon became 20 Euros.

The huge rise in the price of animal feedstuffs and cereals caused by the EU's agricultural policy had already caused inflation with Cyprus' accession to the EU in 2004, but this was intensified with the coming of the Euro in 2008.

As the international financial depression began, Cyprus was already beginning to suffer, which was made worse by the inflation. The arrival of the Euro also led to a huge unsustainable expansion in banking; with Russian money being invested the banks grew beyond their means.

Because the Cyprus economy was small, those bank deposits were invested in Greece. However, when Greece crashed most of those deposits were lost, leading to the events of March 2013, when the Euro group, led by Germany, used Cyprus to teach the "Club Med" countries the facts of life – that Germany was no longer prepared to bail them out and they would have to suffer austerity to save the Euro for the benefit of the northern members of the Euro group.

The net result is that the Cyprus economy will probably shrink by at least 20% by the end of 2014, with the consequential rise in unemployment and misery for the Greek Cypriots.

Recent economy

Cyprus has a free-market, services-based economy, and is one of the most prosperous countries in the Mediterranean region. In the past 20 years, the economy has shifted from agriculture and light manufacturing to services, and the United Nations ranked Cyprus as a "High Potential – High Performer" for future growth.

Before joining the European Union in 2004, Cyprus dismantled most investment restrictions, attracting much foreign investment, particularly from the European Union.

Cyprus has good business and financial services, modern telecommunications, an educated labour force, good airline connections, a sound legal system, and a low crime rate. Cyprus' geographic location, tax incentives and modern infrastructure also make it a natural hub for companies looking to do business with the Middle East, Eastern Europe, the former Soviet Union, the European Union, and North Africa. As a result, Cyprus has developed into an important regional and international business centre.

The GDP in 2009 was $24.7 billion USD. Tourism, the service sector (including financial and health services), industry (mining, manufacturing, chemicals, etc.), and construction, account for the majority of the GDP.

Exports were $1.4 billion in 2009, including agricultural crops, pharmaceuticals, and clothing. Major markets were the European Union (mainly Greece and the U.K.), the Middle East and Russia. Imports were $8.3 billion, including consumer goods, raw materials, petroleum, food, and grains. Major suppliers were Greece, Italy, Germany, and the U.K.

In 2013, the Cyprus government authorised the gas exploration within its own sea boundaries in collaboration with Israel, Syria and Egypt. The Greek Cypriots are hopeful that this exercise will recover the economy to its former level and that as a consequence of the new financial stability the Turkish Cypriots may be tempted in negotiating a solution to the island's partition.

11. OPINION REGARDING TROIKA INTENTIONS

Unintended Consequences

Austerity and 'bail-ins' for depositors and creditors in Cyprus have left the economy in a deeper hole than expected. Experts from the so-called troika of the European Commission, European Central Bank and International Monetary Fund are frequently visiting the Cypriot capital to check on the country's progress in implementing the €10 billion (US$13.2 billion) bailout, which Cyprus reluctantly accepted.

Progress may not be the right word. The economy is forecast by consultancies such as Ernst & Young to shrink by more than 10% by the end of the year, which would be more than the 8.7% forecast by the troika in March, and to continue contracting through 2016. These are the predictable consequences of the experiment its lenders are imposing on Cyprus.

But there are some unpredictable ones too. For the first time since the start of the crisis, a country is being subjected to the bloc's familiar recipe of budget austerity, together with a new dogma of bank "bail-ins," whereby bank creditors or depositors, and not taxpayers, foot the bill for failed banks by forcibly forgoing some of their loans or deposits.

The tiny island has been in financial lockdown for months. For the first time in the 12-year history of the common European currency, capital controls have been imposed to keep cash from fleeing. The conditions for the rescue included the closure of the country's second-largest lender, Cyprus Popular Bank; depositors with more than €100,000 at the bank stand to lose all their money. As well, the largest lender, Bank of Cyprus, is being radically downsized and has been stuck in legal limbo since March, 2013.

Large depositors in Bank of Cyprus do not yet know how much they will lose—their deposits will in part be converted into shares in the bank—though their fate may become clearer as the central bank is expected to make further decisions on the matter. The Cypriots, as well as the international markets, consider the EU approach "nothing short of shock therapy".

The economy's annual output is €16 billion and falling. The government in Nicosia is cutting spending to meet fiscal targets, though forecasts by its international lenders and others suggest this will do nothing to bring down its ballooning debt burden.

With Cyprus Popular Bank shut and Bank of Cyprus downsized, many Cypriot bank depositors have either lost their money or will have to wait to see how much they will get back. As the EU Troika officials sweat into their suits at the height of a Cypriot summer, they may argue that this scale of economic contraction was not part of the design.

But they are discovering another unintended consequence. Politicians from the Euro zone's creditor nations—with bailout-weary voters breathing down their necks—pushed the bail-in idea, declaring they did not intend to use taxpayer money to rescue Russian oligarchs who they alleged were hiding their money in the island's banks.

Based on available data, about half of the deposits in the Bank of Cyprus belonged to non-EU interests, many of which were believed to be Russian. Most of the individual depositors were Cypriots, but the few foreign depositors had far more money in the bank. The bail-in plan will take away part of these deposits and give their owners equity in the new, healthier and leaner bank. A significant share of the bank thus looks likely to end up in Russian hands.

While protesting it did not want to aid the oligarchs—suspecting them of money laundering and other questionable business—the euro zone may have managed to hand them a large slice of the biggest bank in a member state. Russian ownership of the biggest bank in a member state, while unintended, is unlikely to deter the euro zone from enforcing bail-ins in the future. Indeed, EU governments seemed emboldened by the lack of contagion from the Cyprus experiment. Weeks after the bailout, EU governments agreed on rules aimed at making bail-ins the model for dealing with bank failures.

Yet it was Cyprus's small size and isolation that made it easier to prescribe harsh therapy. This depression-inducing combination of austerity and bank bail-ins will not be as easy to impose on larger, better-connected economies.

12. OVERVIEW FOR A SOLUTION

With the Cyprus re-unification negotiations under way since 2008 at an impasse, dramatic steps are needed. As the stalemate continues, the costs for Greek and Turkish Cypriots, Turkey and the European Union (EU) are growing. Neither Greek Cypriots nor Turkish Cypriots can fulfil their potential on an island whose future is divided, uncertain, militarised and facing new economic difficulties.

Turkey's EU candidacy and EU-NATO co-operation, are at risk. Specifically, in order to unblock the situations on the island and in Brussels, the sides should take confidence-building steps in 2013 (unilaterally if necessary) to build trust and satisfy their counterparts' main demands without prejudicing the outcome of a comprehensive settlement.

Interim measures are necessary now, because the UN-facilitated talks look set for another non-productive year. No one wants to incur the stigma of breaking off the talks, so they are likely to stumble on, but a meeting between Secretary-General Ban Ki-moon and the leaders of the two communities failed to signal any new convergence.

Mr Ban Ki-moon was asked by the Security Council to submit an update on the process, following an already critical November 2010 appraisal. Prolonged negotiations make it ever harder to reunify the island, divided politically since Greek Cypriots seized control of the Republic of Cyprus in 1963 and militarily since a Turkish invasion in 1974 created a Turkish Cypriot zone on its northern third.

After nearly four decades, the sides remain far apart even on the meaning of the talks' agreed goal, a bi-zonal, bi-communal federation. While there has long been peace, and relative freedom to interact since 2003, trade and visits between the two communities across the Green Line are decreasing.

Lack of a settlement damages everyone's interests and keeps frustrations high. More than 200,000 Cypriots are still internally displaced persons, and Turkish troops remain in overwhelming force. Few outside the military command in Ankara know if there are 21,000 soldiers, as Turkey says, or 43,000, as Greek Cypriots claim. A dispute that is one indication among many of the distrust and lack of information.

The Turkish Cypriots are cut off from the EU, without the means to trade or travel there directly, though they are EU citizens. The Greek Cypriots have used their membership since 2004 to help bring the EU-Turkey relationship to a standstill, blocking half of the chapters in Turkey's accession negotiations.

Crisis Group has detailed in four reports since 2006 how the interests of the one million Cypriots and outside parties would be best met with a comprehensive political settlement. This remains the ideal, but as it is unrealistic in the coming months, both sides should move ahead with unilateral steps.

The following fourteen points suggested could build confidence and help establish an environment more conducive to an overall agreement:

1. Turkey should open its ports and airports to Greek Cypriot sea and air traffic, meeting its signed 2005 obligation to implement the Additional Protocol to its EU Customs Union, and also permit Greek Cypriot aircraft to transit its airspace,

2. Greek Cypriots should allow the port of Famagusta to handle Cypriot (including Turkish Cypriot) trade with the EU, under Turkish Cypriot management and EU supervision,

3. Greek Cypriots to end their practice of blocking Turkey's EU negotiating chapters,

4. In the event of trade beginning with Turkey after it implements the Additional Protocol, open up the Green Line to the passage of Turkish goods so that Turkish Cypriots can also benefit,

5. Turkey and the Turkish Cypriots should hand back property in the Turkish-military controlled ghost resort of Varosha (Famagusta) to its Greek Cypriot owners, subject to a UN interim regime that oversees reconstruction,

6. The Turkish Armed Forces to return to the Greek Cypriots the educational centres and buildings in Morphou, which they occupied after the invasion,

7. Greek Cypriots should allow charter flights to Ercan Airport in the Turkish Cypriot zone, monitored by the EU,

8. Turkey, Greece, the UK and the two Cypriot communities should put in place a mechanism to verify troop numbers on the island,

9. Similarly, the Turkish Cypriot leadership should organise with Greek Cypriots a census to determine the exact population of the island and the legal status of its inhabitants,

10. Greek Cypriots should co-operate with Turkish Cypriots administrative entities, pending a political settlement,

11. Turkish officials should meet with Greek Cypriot officials and Turkish Cypriots should be supportive,

12. The European Commission, supported by the EU Presidency, should continue to serve as an honest broker to secure agreement on interim steps,

13. Leaders of EU member states should avoid partisan statements at a time when UN talks continue,

14. Political parties of both sides to remain objective during the negotiations and no one party to be obstructive.

These steps are in the interest of all and should be taken unilaterally by the party with the power to do so, not reserved for or made dependent upon negotiated agreements and reciprocity. Some are familiar but have failed because they were bundled into top-heavy negotiated packages, with each side conditioning its one step on two by its counterpart.

Package deals in the Cyprus context have little chance. As recently as the last quarter of 2010, the European Commission and the Belgian EU Presidency tried to facilitate agreement between the Republic of Cyprus and Turkey on a phased opening of sea and airports. This effort should continue under the next EU Presidency.

It is unilateral gestures that have worked in the past, like the Turkish and Turkish Cypriot decision in 2003 to open part of the front lines so Cypriots could cross freely, and the Greek Cypriot decisions since 2004 to offer individual Turkish Cypriots living in the north some citizenship rights, including free health care in 2003 and EU passports since 2004.

The steps proposed would address known needs of the two communities and, far from undermining any party's goals, clear the way for successful negotiations. They would not prejudice the ultimate outcome of talks, or the vexed issue of status, but would help build trust whose absence is a principal reason for four decades of stalemate.

In some cases they would fulfil pledges, like Turkey's obligation to open sea and airports to Greek Cypriot traffic, the EU's promise of direct trade for Turkish Cypriots and Turkey's past agreement to return Famagusta (Varosha) properties before a settlement.

If the status quo continues the following constraints will persist:

1. Greek Cypriots' rejection of the EU-backed UN peace plan will lead to deepening partition,

2. Turkish Cypriots' choice of a hard line will make their territory a backwater of Turkey,

3. Ankara's failure to come to terms with the Greek Cypriots will freeze its EU accession, hurt its reform agenda, prosperity and regional attractiveness,

4. Relationship with Turkey will improve if Greece condemns the high defence budgets and indefinite tensions with Turkey over Aegean Sea demarcation,

5. The European Union will find its soft power diminished by lack of a healthy relationship with its most significant Muslim partner,

6. The European Union must realise that Cyprus will remain an awkward symbol of inability, if they fail to solve the political and military division of a member state.

13. CYPRIOT EURO AND EUROZONE

Recently much has been written about the emerging distinction between the Cypriot Euro and the currency of the Eurozone proper, even though the two are (or were) identical. The argument goes that all €uro's are equal, but those that are found elsewhere than on the doomed island in the eastern Mediterranean are more equal than the Cypriot euros, or something along those lines.

This of course, while superficially right, is woefully inaccurate as it misses the core of the problem, which is a distinction between electronic currency and hard, tangible banknotes. Which is why the capital controls imposed in Cyprus do little to limit the distribution and dissemination of electronic payments within the confines of the island (when it comes to payments leaving the island to other jurisdictions it is a different matter entirely), and are focused exclusively at limiting the procurement and allowance of paper banknotes in the hands of Cypriots (hence the limits on bank branch withdrawals, as well as the hard limit on currency exiting the island).

In other words, what the Cyprus fiasco *should have taught* those lucky enough to be in a net equity position *vis-à-vis* wealth (i.e., have cash savings greater than debts) is that suddenly a €100 banknote is worth far more than €100 in the bank, especially if the €100 is over the insured €100,000 limit.

There is now a very distinct premium to the value of hard cash over electronic cash. While this is true for Euros, it is just as true for US Dollars, Mexican Pesos, Iranian Rials and all other currencies in a fiat regime.

The actual process of money creation takes place primarily in banks to be lent out and re-re-deposited an (un)limited number of times, until there is a literal pyramid of liabilities and obligations lying on top of every dollar, euro, or whatever other currency is in circulation.

The issue is that the bulk of such obligations are electronic, and in its purest form, a bank run such as that seen in Cyprus, and pre-empted with the imposition of the first capital controls in the history of the Eurozone, seeks to convert electronic deposits into hard currency.

What the EU Troika has done to the Cypriot Banks is one of the nastiest and most immoral political acts in modern times.

People, who rob old ladies in the street, or hold up security vans, are branded as thieves. Yet when Germany presides over a heist of billions of pounds from private savers' Cyprus bank accounts, to 'save the euro' for the hundredth time, this is claimed as high statesmanship.

It is nothing of the sort. The deal to secure a €10 billion German bailout of the bankrupt Mediterranean island is one of the nastiest and most immoral political acts of modern times.

It has struck fear into the hearts of hundreds of millions of European citizens, because it establishes a dire precedent.

If democratically elected governments are willing to impose outright confiscation of up to 40 per cent of balances over €100,000 upon depositors in Cyprus, then why not another such hit tomorrow — in Spain, Italy or, most plausibly, Greece?

This is the most brutal display since 2008 of how far the euro-committed nations are willing to go to save the tottering single currency. It shows that the zone's crisis will run and run, to the grievous disadvantage of almost everyone except the Germans.

Berlin insisted upon a harsh line towards the Cypriots because they inhabit a small island with no political influence. Cypriot bankers have behaved with fantastic irresponsibility. They lent huge sums to Greece, and offered high interest rates to dirty money, with no questions asked.

The Germans made it clear that they baulked at providing a cash lifeline to the Russian gangsters who have tried to take over Cyprus with a nod from their friends in the Kremlin.

But hundreds of thousands of honest, decent citizens, including British residents, also had money in the island's banks. They took it for granted that if Cyprus's financial system was deemed worthy to be part of the Eurozone, it must be as safe as the Bundesbank.

They were fully entitled to make that assumption, and to be outraged by the looting of their accounts today.

The fact that the major European countries consider Cyprus to be a rackety semi-gangster society made it madness ever to allow the island to join the Eurozone, rather than an excuse, as now, for stealing its citizens' money.

The Germans, who effectively control and bankroll the whole single-currency system, acted recklessly by signing on Cyprus — and Greece, Italy, Portugal, Spain and Ireland. None of these countries had economic convergence with northern Europe.

But Berlin chose to pretend that they did, because it thus became enormously profitable for Germany to trade with them in an undervalued common currency rather than a sky-high Deutschmark.

It always appeared absurd for the Germans, who (like the British) obey rules, pay taxes and tell the truth in financial documents, to form a financial union with the southern Europeans, who do none of those things, and are never likely to.

Incredibly, there is a real prospect that Silvio Berlusconi will be able to form a new Italian coalition government, even though a string of court verdicts has found him to be a major criminal with a repulsive record of sexual behaviour.

How can the rest of Europe do serious business with a country that wilfully chooses to be led by such a man? Many Italians find this acceptable, and somehow make it work. But the Italian way, like the Cypriot and Greek way, is not our way. The Germans, by trying to pretend otherwise, are defying gravity.

More than two years ago now, a senior central banker flatly declare that the Eurozone is unsustainable. He has repeated the same view every time he is interviewed. He believes that if the southern Europeans left the system, after a period of turmoil they might be amazed how quickly they can restore themselves to prosperity, once they can trade in their own heavily devalued currencies.

But he has always believed that if, alternatively, the southern Europeans attempt to cling on in the euro, the consequence will be an interminable crisis, with unending austerity imposing huge and perhaps un-containable social and political strains; riots on the streets.

What have the Cypriot people now got to look forward to, save the ruin of their economy along with their banking system, its principal engine? Who will ever trust money to a Cyprus bank again?

Any tourist who has bought a cup of coffee in Italy, Greece or Spain in the past few years knows how fantastically high those countries' cost of living is. Yet they stagger blindly on, stubbornly seeking to pretend that they can play with the big boys, share a currency with mighty Germany. This masquerade may continue for years, with France joining the ranks of the economic basket-cases, because its government, too, rejects economic reality.

Even though Britain is not in the euro, what is happening has immense implications for the United Kingdom. As long as the European economies remain stagnant, conditions will remain tough here, because so much of British trade is with Europe.

Moreover, the Cyprus precedent is as scary for people who live in Slough as for those who live in Limassol. Almost every Western society, including Britain, is burdened with debt it cannot ever realistically hope to pay off. There are only three ways in which governments can get off the hook: taxation, inflation and confiscation. The current British Coalition is playing with only the first two of these.

But Ed Miliband, Ed Balls and Nick Clegg are openly wedded to a mansion tax, which, if introduced, would be no more and no less an act of highway robbery than the Cypriot so-called 'haircut' on bank deposits. Having adopted the principle that it is morally acceptable to seize a proportion of citizens' assets, they are on the road to a Cypriot position; a Cypriot solution.

Germany still has a stubborn, visceral belief that the euro can be preserved in its present form, along with its own economic and political dominance of Europe.

Berlin's rulers seem willing to pay almost any price to achieve this, though it shall be discovered at the country's next elections whether their voters feel the same way.

The spectacle of the richest nation in Europe foreclosing on one of the smallest, looting the savings of thousands of people, is profoundly repugnant.

Surely the euro cannot long survive by such anti-democratic means. It certainly does not deserve to.

EU & Germany robbing Cyprus

END

14. BIBLIOGRAPHY

TITLES PUBLISHED BY ANDREAS SOFRONIOU
AND USED AS BIBLIOGRAPHY IN THIS BOOK

FICTION & POETRY

1. THE TOWERING MISFEASANCE, ISBN: 978-1-4241-3652-0
2. DANCES IN THE MOUNTAINS – THE BEAUTY AND BRUTALITY, ISBN: 978-1-4092-7674-6
3. YUSUF'S ODYSSEY, ISBN: 978-1-291-33902-4
4. WILD AND FREE, ISBN: 978-1-4452-0747-6
5. HATCHED FREE, ISBN: 978-1-291-37668-5
6. THROUGH PRICKLY SHRUBS, ISBN: 978-1-4092-7439-1
7. BLOOMIN' SLUMS, ISBN: 978-1-291-37662-3
8. SPEEDBALL, ISBN: 978-1-4092-0521-0
9. SPIRALLING ADVERSARIES, ISBN: 978-1-291-35449-2
10. EXULTATION, ISBN: 978-1-4092-7483-4
11. FREAKY LANDS, ISBN: 978-1-4092-7603-6
12. LITTLE HUT BY THE SEA, ISBN: 978-1-4478-4066-4
13. THE SAME RIVER TWICE, ISBN: 978-1-4457-1576-6
14. THE CANE HILL EFFECT, ISBN: 978-1-4452-7636-6
15. WINDS OF CHANGE, ISBN: 978-1-4452-4036-7
16. A TOWN CALLED MORPHOU, ISBN: 978-1-4092-7611-1
17. EXPERIENCE MY BEFRIENDED IDEAL, ISBN: 978-1-4092-7463-6
18. MAN AND HIS MULE, ISBN: 978-1-291-27090-7

EDUCATION & PHILOSOPHY

19. MORAL PHILOSOPHY, FROM SOCRATES TO THE 21ST AEON, ISBN: 978-1-4457-4618-0
20. MORAL PHILOSOPHY, FROM HIPPOCRATES TO THE 21ST AEON, ISBN: 978-1-84753-463-7
21. THERAPEUTIC PHILOSOPHY FOR THE INDIVIDUAL AND THE STATE, ISBN: 978-1-4092-7586-2
22. PHILOSOPHIC COUNSELLING FOR PEOPLE AND THEIR GOVERNMENTS, ISBN: 978-1-4092-7400-1
23. MORAL PHILOSOPHY, THE ETHICAL APPROACH THROUGH THE AGES, ISBN: 978-1-4092-7703-3
24. MORAL PHILOSOPHY, ISBN: 978-1-4478-5037-3
25. PSYCHOANALYSIS, POETRY, ISBN: 978-1-4467-2741-6

26. PLATO'S EPISTEMOLOGY, ISBN: 978-1-4716-6584-4
27. ARISTOTLE'S AETIOLOGY, ISBN: 978-1-4716-7861-5
28. MARXISM, SOCIALISM & COMMUNISM, ISBN: 978-1-4716-8236-0
29. MACHIAVELLI'S POLITICS & RELEVANT PHILOSOPHICAL CONCEPTS, ISBN: 978-1-4716-8629-0
30. BRITISH PHILOSOPHERS, 16TH TO 18TH CENTURY, ISBN: 978-1-4717-1072-8
31. ROUSSEAU ON WILL AND MORALITY, ISBN: 978-1-4717-1070-4
32. HEGEL ON IDEALISM, KNOWLEDGE & REALITY, ISBN: 978-1-4717-0954-8
33. PHILOLOGY, CONCEPTS OF EUROPEAN LITERATURE, ISBN: 978-1-291-49148-7
34. THREE MILLENNIA OF HELLENIC PHILOLOGY, ISBN: 978-1291-49799-1
35. CYPRUS, PERMANENT DEPRIVATION OF FREEDOM, ISBN: 978-1-291-50833-8

MEDICINE & PSYCHOLOGY

36. MEDICAL ETHICS THROUGH THE AGES, ISBN: 978-1-4092-7468-1
37. MEDICAL ETHICS, FROM HIPPOCRATES TO THE 21ST CENTURY ISBN: 978-1-4457-1203-1
38. THE MISINTERPRETATION OF SIGMUND FREUD, ISBN: 978-1-4467-1659-5
39. JUNG'S PSYCHOTHERAPY: THE PSYCHOLOGICAL & MYTHOLOGICAL METHODS, ISBN: 978-1-4477-4740-6
40. FREUDIAN ANALYSIS & JUNGIAN SYNTHESIS, ISBN: 978-1-4477-5996-6
41. PSYCHOLOGY FROM CONCEPTION TO SENILITY, ISBN: 978-1-4092-7218-2
42. PSYCHOTHERAPY, CONCEPTS OF TREATMENT, ISBN: 978-1-291-50178-0
43. PSYCHOLOGY, CONCEPTS OF BEHAVIOUR, ISBN: 978-1-291-47573-9
44. PSYCHOLOGY OF CHILD CULTURE, ISBN: 978-1-4092-7619-7
45. JOYFUL PARENTING, ISBN: 0 9527956 1 2
46. THE GUIDE TO A JOYFUL PARENTING, ISBN: 0 952 7956 1 2
47. PHILOSOPHY FOR HUMAN BEHAVIOUR, ISBN: 978-1-291-12707-2

INFORMATION TECHNOLOGY & MANAGEMENT

48. I.T. RISK MANAGEMENT, ISBN: 978-1-4467-5653-9
49. SYSTEMS ENGINEERING, ISBN: 978-1-4477-7553-9
50. BUSINESS INFORMATION SYSTEMS, CONCEPTS AND EXAMPLES, ISBN:

978-1-4092-7338-7

51. A GUIDE TO INFORMATION TECHNOLOGY, ISBN: 978-1-4092-7608-1
52. CHANGE MANAGEMENT IN I.T., ISBN: 978-1-4092-7712-5
53. FRONT-END DESIGN AND DEVELOPMENT FOR SYSTEMS APPLICATIONS, ISBN: 978-1-4092-7588-6
54. I.T RISK MANAGEMENT, ISBN: 978-1-4092-7488-9
55. THE SIMPLIFIED PROCEDURES FOR I.T. PROJECTS DEVELOPMENT, ISBN: 978-1-4092-7562-6
56. THE SIGMA METHODOLOGY FOR RISK MANAGEMENT IN SYSTEMS DEVELOPMENT, ISBN: 978-1-4092-7690-6
57. TRADING ON THE INTERNET IN THE YEAR 2000 AND BEYOND, ISBN: 978-1-4092- 7577
58. STRUCTURED SYSTEMS METHODOLOGY, ISBN: 978-1-4477-6610-0
59. INFORMATION TECHNOLOGY LOGICAL ANALYSIS, ISBN: 978-1-4717-1688-1
60. I.T. RISKS LOGICAL ANALYSIS, ISBN: 978-1-4717-1957-8
61. I.T. CHANGES LOGICAL ANALYSIS, ISBN: 978-1-4717-2288-2
62. LOGICAL ANALYSIS OF SYSTEMS, RISKS , CHANGES, ISBN: 978-1-4717-2294-3
63. COMPUTING, A PRÉCIS ON SYSTEMS, SOFTWARE AND HARDWARE, ISBN: 978-1-2910-5102-5
64. MANAGE THAT I.T. PROJECT, ISBN: 978-1-4717-5304-6
65. CHANGE MANAGEMENT, ISBN: 978-1-4457-6114-5
66. MANAGEMENT OF I.T. CHANGES, RISKS, WORKSHOPS, EPISTEMOLOGY, ISBN: 978-1-84753-147-6
67. THE MANAGEMENT OF COMMERCIAL COMPUTING, ISBN: 978-1-4092-7550-3
68. PROGRAMME MANAGEMENT WORKSHOP, ISBN: 978-1-4092-7583-1
69. THE PHILOSOPHICAL CONCEPTS OF MANAGEMENT THROUGH THE AGES, ISBN: 978-1-4092- 7554-1
70. THE MANAGEMENT OF PROJECTS, SYSTEMS, INTERNET, AND RISKS, ISBN: 978-1-4092- 7464-3
71. HOW TO CONSTRUCT YOUR RESUMÊ, ISBN: 978-1-4092-7383-7
72. DEFINE THAT SYSTEM, ISBN: 978-1-291-15094-0
73. INFORMATION TECHNOLOGY WORKSHOP, ISBN: 978-1-291-16440-4
74. CHANGE MANAGEMENT IN SYSTEMS, ISBN: 978-1-4457-1099-0
75. SYSTEMS MANAGEMENT, ISBN: 978-1-4710-4907-1

www.ingramcontent.com/pod-product-compliance
Lightning Source LLC
Chambersburg PA
CBHW070836310526
45788CB00017B/1323